HOSPITALITY MARKETING

HOSPITALITY MARKETING

Harish Bhatt

CRESCENT
PUBLISHING CORPORATION

[The responsibility for the facts stated, conclusions reached and plagiarism, if any, in this book is entirely that of the Author. And the Publisher bears no responsibility for them, whatsoever.]

Hospitality Marketing

First Published : 2006

ISBN 81-8342-003-6

Published by :

CRESCENT PUBLISHING CORPORATION
4831/24, Prahlad Street,
Ansari Road, Darya Ganj,
New Delhi - 110002
Ph. : 23272541, 23257835
Fax : 91- 011- 23257835
e-mail : campusbooks@hotmail.com

Typesetting by :

Arjun Computers
Delhi - 110051

Printed at :
S.P. Printech
Delhi

Preface

As a business that has always been driven by customer demand, cyclical periods of downturns and upturns are not new to the hospitality industry. However, the industry, which is composed of mainly small and medium-sized enterprises, is now in a period of profound transition. In recent years, it has been adapting to rapid technological change moving methodically toward the internet as a distribution system of information and communication. Most hospitality marketing managers are uncertain of their approach to developing a convenient, information-rich and value -adding web presence harnessed to a booking engine, an increasingly critical e-business requirement.

As new marketing strategies have becomes increasingly important to the success of today's businesses, the present volume gives, students of hospitality profession, an important career-building resource for virtually every area of the field. It features plain language explanations, demanding exercises, and solid reinforcement of underlying theory to give students a firm grasp of the fundamentals as they explore the intricacies of marketing in this complex and rapidly growing industry. With cutting-edge information and a strong emphasis on real-world applications, it gives aspiring hospitality professionals the knowledge, experience, and confidence they will need to meet the challenges of this dynamic and rewarding industry.

Harish Bhatt

Contents

1

Functions of Hospitality Marketing

Marketing is every kind of contact an activity has with potential patrons which brings them into an activity, satisfies them, and keeps them. Marketing is an on-going, patron-driven process that requires determining patron needs and desires and then delivering programs and/or services to meet those needs and desires.

To provide your patrons with the product or program they desire, you must consider the marketing mix, or the four "P's" which are the basic functions of marketing-product, price, place, and promotion.

Product : A product may be defined as a thing produced by an action, operation, or labor; a result. A product should include a set of intangible, psychological attributes as well as the tangible end product. Some examples of intangible attributes are convenience, taste, and satisfaction to the customer. Your goal should be to offer the product that gives your customers their desired product attributes and level of quality.

Price: Price is the value assigned to something bought, sold, or offered for sale. The value must include the way a market responds to price. To determine the best price, you can rely on one or both of these two methods: cost-plus and/or demand-oriented. The cost-plus method requires a knowledge of various types of costs: fixed costs, variable costs, and total costs. The demand-oriented method requires knowledge of this data and knowledge of what your market is willing to pay for your product. You assign the price at which your customers will purchase your product.

*Place:*Place, in marketing terms, encompasses distribution channels and the method used to distribute your product. You must distribute (sell) your product in the areas where there is demand for it. Your product should also be available when it is desired. An example of "place" is distributing hamburgers in a restaurant and not in a department store.

Promotion: You can conduct a great market analysis, develop the best product, and set the right price; but if customers are not aware of your product, all your efforts are in vain. Promotion is the process of informing customers of availability and convincing them to buy. To state this more simply-promotion is telling and selling.

Marketing Functions

Food and Hospitality managers must become more scientific and businesslike in their methods to meet the objectives of satisfying patron's needs and profitability. Practicing the functions of marketing will help reach these objectives. The functions of marketing, which will be addressed separately throughout this NAVMC, include:

— Marketing Research, the primary tool for determining the true needs and desires of patrons.

— Promotion, for communicating to patrons, which includes advertising, public relations, publicity, and selling.

— Marketing Planning, provides a logical, business-based sense of direction for your activity.

Food and hospitality managers must realize that patrons have numerous options available to them during their disposable time, and MWR is in competition for that time. In other words, the base restaurant is in competition with more than other off-base restaurants. The marketing process provides management with specific information about the patron and non-patron. It is the information that allows management to target specific groups towards specific programs.

The marketing process provides the data for planning program objectives; i.e., hours of operation, number of employees, types of equipment needed, patron likes and dislikes, etc. Above all, by using marketing principles, management can promote the benefits of patronizing the activity. When the patron needs correlate with benefits and the perceived value of participation, the potential for increased usage exists.

Marketing Research

Managers can no longer just open the doors to a facility and expect patrons to flock in. Numerous surveys have repeatedly identified that it is not unusual for our MWR patrons to willingly pay more for an off-base service or activity, even when the same service is offered on base.

Historically, a major problem for MWR is that programming has often been a management decision. That is, management decides what activities to offer, hours of operation, etc., instead of basing program decisions on the wants and needs of the patron. A good example is the selection of entertainment or type of music offered in the club. In many instances "someone" in MWR will make the decision to offer whatever their preference is, without any input from patrons. At showtime, the club is only half full and the organizers cannot understand why. Formal surveys or informal questionnaires, in addition to analysis of past usage data, may have pointed out that the majority of patrons wanted rock n' roll instead of Rap. Unfortunately, this type of planning and analysis was not used when management selected the band or D.J. Although the band may be excellent, if it is not what the patrons want, the performance may be canceled for lack of interest.

Market research will help identify your patron's needs and desires. Research methods include questionnaires, formal surveys, participant comment cards, focus groups, and informal observation. Once the decision is made to conduct research, the first step is to determine exactly what type of information is needed. Sample question areas are:

— Who are the current users of the facility? (i.e., rank, gender, live on or off base, household size, income)

— When do the majority of the patrons use a specific facility? (which day of the week and what time of day)

— What types of programs do the majority of patrons desire? (active or passive)

— Why does the patron participate? (benefits of program)

— What are the users' attitudes toward programming? (satisfied versus unsatisfied)

Research Methods

There are numerous methods available to management for conducting marketing research. Some of the methods are ongoing processes while others are for a specific length of time. The more familiar techniques include:

— *Asking:* Patrons and potential patrons should routinely be asked about their likes, dislikes, desires, and needs concerning the food and hospitality program. MWR personnel should seek information form both users and non-users. Many civilian-sector restaurants, clubs, and hotels make calls to their patrons to find out their feelings about services offered.

— *Observing:* The employees and activity manager should observe patrons. Observation can provide many clues about levels of satisfaction and usage.

— Suggestion Boxes: The suggestion box is a useful and effective management tool if used correctly. The boxes should be located in high traffic areas, must be well maintained, and have paper and pencils available. To further elicit patron participation, patron comments should be acted upon and the action publicized.

— *After-Action Reports:* Evaluating after-action reports received from activity and program managers can be helpful for planning future activities. By preparing in-depth reports, mistakes can be avoided and new personnel will not have to reinvent the wheel each time a program is offered. Historically, after-action reports have helped in assessing trends and predicting future programming needs.

— *Questionnaires:* There are two types of questionnaires, informal and formal, that can elicit vital information from patrons.

— *Informal Questionnaires:* These surveys can be accomplished on the spot (intercept interviews) and do not utilize the scientific method. Informal questionnaires should be kept as short as possible and are meant to be given to patrons while they are participating in an activity or shortly thereafter. They should not cause the patron any inconvenience.

Although an informal questionnaire does not provide scientific data, it does provide information about the patron's attitude towards the program. Furthermore, if this survey is accomplished "on the spot" the information gained from the patron is timely and accurate because the experience is still vivid in the patron's mind. Specific trends are also easily noted if the information is analyzed immediately.

Promotion Strategies

Promotion is the process of communicating between your activity and your eligible patrons, the media, other agencies, your command, your management, and staff. Promotion consists of informing, persuading, and influencing the patron. It increases awareness and understanding and allows patrons to become more knowledgeable and thus more discriminating. Through promotion, you can inform patrons of the benefits your activity offers, and how your activity is distinctively different from other similar establishments.

Why is promotion important? While we may assume that word-of-mouth is the way the majority of patrons find out about MWR activities, it is nonetheless important that certain methods be used to provide first-hand information. The assumption regarding word-of-mouth, however, may be flawed. On most military installations the physical distance, social structure, and psychological perceptions of MWR may create barriers that often cannot be changed by word-of-mouth alone. Low quality brochures or flyers give the impression that management really doesn't care about image, thereby creating a negative impression toward the program.

To make promotion decisions, you should cover at least four areas:

(1) define the product characteristics

(2) establish promotion objectives

(3) determine the nature of the message, including timing and frequency

(4) determine the promotion-mix patterns which will effectively and efficiently deliver the message. By systematically approaching this decision process, your chances to maximize success will be increased.

Food and hospitality and marketing managers, working together, can develop the most successful promotion and communication program. A number of promotional methods should be used, and to be effective, promotions must be constantly repeated. In the commercial sector, a message is repeated at least six times before the individual is motivated to either visit a hotel or go to a restaurant.

Types of promotional tools

There are many ways to promote your program. Try to vary the types of promotional tools you use for different events or activities. Some of the promotional tools you have at your disposal include:

Advertising

Advertising is a method of communicating with consumers, and is used to stimulate repeat business, introduce new services, and announce any changes in regular services and/or facilities. It is usually accomplished through newspapers, magazines, brochures, flyers, radio, and television. The primary objective of advertising is to keep patrons aware of club services and programs. It is especially important that advertising be used frequently since there are many potential patrons arriving on the base daily and for short periods of duty. Food and hospitality activities cannot rely on their past reputation because of this high turnover.

The second objective of advertising is to provide a favorable image of club offerings. This may also be referred to as the "soft sell" approach. The objective is not to sell specific services or programs through advertising, but rather to sell by advertising the activity itself. For example, the Temporary Lodging Facility (TLF) might distribute a brochure stating the facility's location, along with some simple remark such as: "If you are expecting out-of-town guests, think of us." No specific products or services are mentioned; it is merely a notice of the TLF's availability.

The third objective is often referred to as "pre-sell." This occurs when there are specific promotions, specials, or benefits that are to be communicated. The "pre-sell" objective is applied to advertising which is aimed at inducing immediate action. A special limited time offer and special one-night entertainment are examples of this approach.

It is important to remember tnese objectives before implementing an advertising program. Each program will have its particular requirements and, in order to be effective, should be specific in nature according to its purpose.

There are two strategies in advertising, direct and indirect.

— *Direct advertising* is when the patron is encouraged to immediately take advantage of a service. For example, if food and hospitality has a promotion scheduled for a limited time, direct advertisements should stress that the timeliness of the promotion is critical. Direct advertising is intense over a limited period of time.

— *Indirect advertising,* however, attempts to create a long-range demand for the service. This method instills in patrons the knowledge that a service or program is available if and when they are interested in pursuing it. For example, if the Enlisted Club has Happy Hour every Friday throughout the year, or offers check cashing, indirect advertising is the method that should be used to promote this particular offering.

Public Relations

Public relations (PR) refers to the total image projected by an organization. Efforts that establish, maintain, and improve activity image are all part of PR, and consist of advertising, packaging, customer relations, and corporate policy. For food and hospitality, PR involves the creation of a positive patron attitude and goodwill toward the activity. The day-to-day image conveyed through employees, management practices, and the physical facility is more important than any other advertising and is essential to success. An activity's perceived image can attract or turn away potential patrons.

Sales Promotion

This technique is designed to stimulate patron involvement in programs food and hospitality activities wish to promote.

There are at least four types of sales promotion. They are:

— *Sampling:* This is an attempt to pre-sell the activity and/or service to the patron. For example, the base restaurant may want to promote a new dessert menu by providing an opportunity for patrons to sample a small piece of the "dessert of the evening", free of charge. This gives patrons a chance to sample the food with the idea that they will like it and be influenced to purchase it, or another dessert, the next time they dine at the restaurant.

— *Coupons:* Coupons are used by 70 percent of American retailers in promoting products. Some commands provide MWR coupons good for reduced charges at MWR activities to stimulate interest and participation. Couponing has yet to reach its full impact. A coupon gives the patron the opportunity to participate in an activity at reduced or no cost. They can be very effective with new personnel assigned to the command, used as a motivational tool for them to visit your activity.

— *Contests:* A contest may be used as a promotional method directed toward creating additional enthusiasm and interest. Contests usually provide some form of prizes. An example of a contest to promote enthusiasm and interest in a particular activity is a chili cook-off, held at the snackbar, judged by your staff, and a featured menu for a period of time, in hopes that the contest will encourage patrons to visit the snackbar more often.

— *Demonstrations:* To create interest in your menu specialties or new Chef, a cooking demonstration might be arranged to take place at the exchange mall or at a booth during an MWR festival.

Personal Selling

Perhaps the most under-utilized method in the delivery of the MWR message is personal selling. All food and hospitality personnel should be knowledgeable about what other activities have to offer. When a patron visits one activity, there should be information available that makes the patron aware of other activities. Many commands have the MWR Director or other staff member brief personnel at welcome aboard or training briefs. These are perfect opportunities to not only talk about what food and hospitality offers, but also to "sell" the entire program.

Personal selling leaves a lasting impression because of the person-to-person contact. The main implication of personal selling is that each employee must be activity and patron oriented, and must make every effort to provide the patron with efficient, friendly, courteous service. Skillful personal selling is not something that can be taught to an employee easily-it is an attitude. But it is something that can be influenced through training and good staff relations.

It is impossible to have good personal selling if the management and staff are not proud of their activity and its services. Management cannot expect the staff to be sales people unless they have a good reason to be proud of their work. It is a combination, therefore, of both the management and the staff that accounts for successful selling. Each must accept personal responsibility for promoting the club in the course of their daily job related activities.

Public Speaking

Public speaking offers another opportunity to sell your activity. Presentations to wives' clubs, incoming Marines, and at social functions can inform, influence, and stimulate interest in MWR activities. The use of slides, movies, and other visual cues can enhance the effectiveness of the presentation. The person speaking should be well prepared and keep the presentation well paced and interesting. Let all base activities and local organizations know you are available as a speaker.

Private and base organizations may welcome you as a speaker at their meetings, especially if you have an exhibit or demonstration to present. Outreach to the local community provides an excellent opportunity to get acquainted and become knowledgeable about local demographics. Briefings should be given periodically to all commands, staff personnel, appropriate clubs, and base organizations.

Promotional Media

Various forms of media can be used to promote and communicate your program or a promotion to potential patrons. Some of the most important are as follows:

— *Brochures:* Brochures can provide patrons information about food and hospitality activities, facilities, and services. A brochure may be current for a limited duration, such as one which promotes a specific promotion; or it may be timeless, such as one which indicates facility location, hours of operation, services offered, etc.

  There is a wide variety of creative ideas which can be used when developing brochures. Some helpful guidelines are:

  — Use two color paper for interest and black ink for impact.

— Medium weight paper is more impressive than light weight.

— Consider the different paper textures available, such as matte or glossy.

— Bi-fold and three-fold are the most common type of folds used.

— Photos create interest.

— Areas of white space encourage reading.

— Set off headlines by using larger type and/or different typefaces, such as bold and italics.

— Indent paragraphs.

— *Flyers:* Should be thought of as miniature posters that highlight important details of a program, service, or activity. Key elements to consider in developing an effective flyer are:

— Accuracy

— Quality

— Logo

— White space

— Who, What, Where, When, Why, and How

— Large letters for easy reading

— Rub-on letters instead of a felt pen

— Blowup of photo for background

— Silk screening

Remember to remove all brochures and posters when they become out-of-date.

— *Marquees:* Marquees, billboards, and signs are on duty 24 hours a day and are an excellent complement to existing advertising. One of the primary considerations in setting up a billboard or marquee is location. Criteria for determining placement:

  — Length of unobstructed view. When does the sign become fully visible from a car?

  — Type of traffic. Fast? Slow?

  — Does the sign face oncoming or outgoing traffic?

  — Immediate surroundings. Are there traffic lights, competing signs, buildings?

  — Size and physical appeal of the sign.

  — Patrons to be reached. Do you want to contact patrons going to or from work?

  Marquees must be easy to read. Keep the message short-eight words or less and if possible include the MWR logo. Marquees are usually read as the patron is moving, so they must say only one thing and say it clearly. The clarity and aesthetics are also important in telling the patron what type of operation you have. A good looking sign connotes a quality operation. A key element relating to the patron's awareness is keeping the message on the marquee current. Messages should be changed every few days to keep the patron's interest. Old messages result in patrons losing interest and reduces the overall effectiveness of the marquee.

— *Posters:* Posters should be large, eye-catching, and easy to read and understand. Produce enough to distribute to all base activities, and if possible, post outside as well as inside. Place the posters in high-traffic areas, and if there are no bulletin boards available, use easels to display your message.

— *Activity Calendars:* Send calendars to target groups featuring activities they are most likely to participate in. This is an excellent means of providing patrons with a long-range schedule of upcoming events, programs, etc.

— *Audio Visuals:* Videotapes, slide shows, and other visual media can effectively present your message. These can be used for welcome aboard briefs, command cable television, base community meetings (such as wives' clubs), or as movie trailers at the base theater. Audio visuals should be made available to every pertinent activity, both on and off base.

— *Other Visuals:* Banners are excellent for advertising upcoming events. Hang them in high traffic areas such as main gates and use large letters on both sides and consider silk-screening, hand lettering, and Velcro letters. Bus Cards used inside base buses, similar to those seen in subways and on commercial buses, are effective because they have a captive audience. Signs on the back and sides of MWR vehicles will attract attention. Exhibits presenting a specific activity are an excellent way to elicit interest and attract new patrons. For example, an appealing, eye-catching exhibit about your activity and located in the exchange area, can encourage people to visit your activity. Buttons, T-shirt messages, table tents, menu clip-ons, and messages on place mats, napkins, and coasters will call attention to your activity message. Work with other base facilities to get your message to their patrons and participants.

— *Telephone Hot Lines:* You can designate a special number to call for information about MWR activities.

All announcements on the pre-recorded telephone message should include upcoming events, discount information, MWR news, local entertainment, schedules, etc. If you use a recorded message, make sure the information is current. Make sure there is someone available to answer calls and the line is relatively free from other types of incoming calls. Publicize the number as much as possible.

— *Direct Mailings:* The greatest advantage of direct mail advertising is that it will reach the intended market. For direct mail advertising purposes, you can strive to reach your basic markets. Your basic markets are: active duty Marines and their families, retired military, reservists in your area, and other eligible MWR patrons, such as civilians who work on base. From a direct mail standpoint the markets do not need to be further segmented. The effectiveness of direct mail advertising depends on current lists and addresses of potential and current patrons. This includes timely information for all Recent arrivals. As an example you may want to send a personalized welcome aboard letter. The letter should be sent to newly arrived Marines and their families, inviting them to visit food and hospitality activities. It could serve as the only nice individualized touch that the newcomer receives.

Many other types of information can be communicated through direct mail; such as special promotions, menus, parties, and entertainment. It is important that direct mail advertisements be kept separate from the monthly newsletter since the advertisement loses its effectiveness when it accompanies regularly delivered material.

Direct mail advertisements should be creative, professionally presented, and informative. The date, time, location, price, and other necessary information describing the special promotions should always be included. It is also a good idea to have the promoter (manager, chef, assistant) personally sign the direct mail advertisement before mailing. This adds a special extra touch. It becomes a personal invitation rather than a general invitation.

There are three major concerns associated with direct mail advertising. First, care should be taken not to overstuff direct mail advertisements with more than one or two promotions. The more stuffing, the less likelihood of its being read. Second, care must be taken to personalize the mail as much as possible (i.e., ink signed letter versus stamped); and third, the material should be professional in appearance. The cost of direct mail advertising may be one of the most effective advertising expenditures that an activity can make. It is sent specifically to the primary patron and is utilized only when something special is being promoted. Each food and hospitality manager should incorporate direct mail advertising into the marketing budget.

— *Newspapers:* The base paper is perhaps the most effective method of communication used by MWR activities. At many installations, MWR writes their own news releases and provides the information to Public Affairs. Well written newspaper articles usually describe what the activity is, where it will be held, when it will take place, what the cost will be, and to whom the services are directed. The first paragraph of the news release should include information such as who, what, why, when, and where. Use "how" in the second paragraph if it will not fit easily into the first.

News releases are cut away from the bottom up by editors, so make the first paragraph the most substantive and the last paragraph the least important, with the others providing information and data to support the lead paragraph. Use only as much material as will fit on one sheet of paper, double space, with one inch wide margins. Use clear, concise language and get to the point. If possible, use a quote from a dignitary, an official or a base officer to lend creditability and another angle to stories. The newspaper can expand the story by calling the appropriate contact person for more information.

— *MWR Supplements:* Supplements are an excellent means of providing informative articles and ads to a widespread audience. This publication is produced periodically and provides readers with an in-depth look at a particular program, special event, discount attraction, etc.

Creating Effective Promotional Copy

When writing promotional material remember these basic rules:

— Get peoples' attention.

— Show people an advantage.

— Prove it.

— Persuade people to take the advantage.

— Call for action.

Get Attention

Capture the interest of your prospective readers by making your material arresting and eye catching, but don't get "arty." On flyers and posters use white space as part of your total design because too much art work can be distracting and can take away from your message. Try to get a base or local area professional, or talented amateur, to create your message, your flyers, and posters. Don't confuse your reader with too much information, but make sure you are specific about who, what, when, and where. Do not assume that the reader knows what you already know. Be clear and concise and give just enough information to accomplish your objective. You do not want to overwhelm your readers in copy or graphics. Make your first sentence or headline a "grabber." The best grabbers create a picture in the mind of the reader and arouse interest.

Show People an Advantage

People want to know what your activity will do for them. Concentrate on that. Show them in words, in pictures, or both, what they can save, gain, or accomplish. Make sure that your message is stated in terms your audience can understand. Write your copy for them and not for yourself.

Prove It

If you have a reputation for delivering what you promise, this is easy. Direct mail promotions have room to state facts to back up your claims. For posters and other promotional mediums, this information should be as brief and clear as possible. Another way to "prove it" is to remind people of past activities or events that were successful. Posters can use an enlarged photograph of a previous similar activity that went well. You can use tag reminders like: "By request we've brought back . . ." or "You liked (--), so now . . ." Photos can be used in a feature story for the newspaper. If you make any sort of guarantee, be prepared to back it up and deliver on it.

Persuade People to Take Advantage

Make your copy timely and make an offer that needs to be acted on soon. Offer a booklet, a sample, or some other inducement to motivate action. Put a time limit on your offer. State that the supply is limited. Show what can be lost by not acting: "A special night out that won't empty the piggybank ... $3.00 off dinner-for-two and a bottle of wine." "THIS WEEK ONLY"

Call for Action

Use words that telegraph action "Write Now," "Call Today," "Sign Up Now." Give an address as well as a telephone number if possible. Having to call to find out additional information is an "interim action." It is an additional step people must take before they can act on your suggestions. Try to keep them from having to take any additional steps. Keep the address simple so that it will be easily remembered by using a building number or a base landmark (i.e., snackbar located in the Exchange mall). Do whatever is necessary to make sure action can be taken in a simple and easy way.

Visual Aids

Photographs: Photographs are excellent to use in flyers1 brochures, and other media. Subjects should appear relaxed and natural and the settings should be pleasant. However, no smile at all is better than a stiff smile or a false smile. Shoot candid shots so people look more natural and interesting. If the photo must be posed, give your subjects something to do or hold, and take the shot as they are talking, or examining something, this makes a more relaxed picture.

Important points to remember about photographs are:

— Take your photographs from more than one angle.

— Action shots that are not posed are more interesting than planned "action" shots which very often have an artificial/posed quality to them.

— Keep the background on still shots simple. Where possible, avoid more than two or three people in a photograph. Avoid patterned wallpaper, lots of background activity, trees, and potted palms "growing" out of your subject's head. Pay close attention to details. Remove sunglasses and drinking glasses, and make sure cigars and cigarettes are being held and not puffed. Straighten ties and lookout for rumpled clothing.

— If you are photographing an event, take your picture being mindful that your action photographs could be used in brochures, enlarged for posters or display boards, and used as slides. Try to get action shots in 35mm, and use color as well as the black and white film necessary for newspaper photographs.

— Start a photograph file. The file will be available for you to draw from whenever you need a photograph for a brochure or a special promotional activity. Take your pictures with your photo file in mind.

— Never photograph rooms, halls, lobbies or any other physical portion of your facilities or operation empty of people or with only a few people in a vast area. The general effect will be lonesome and forlorn no matter how splendid the decorations or equipment shown. If you plan to take such photographs, be sure there are enough people in the picture that the effect is one of a pleasant, well-used atmosphere, but not so crowded as to be uncomfortable.

— Do not pose your models; such photographs will always look rigid. Instead, have them actually dancing in the club bar among the new decorations. Take your photographs after your models are relaxed and have begun to enjoy themselves; that enjoyment will come across in your photographs. This is one of those situations where you may want to have two or three photographers present to take shots from different angles.

— Photograph prints should be made on glossy paper, 8" x 10" preferably, but 5" x 7" is often used. Check with your base newspaper and other possible outlets for your photographs to see what is preferred.

— Photograph Captions: Every photograph must have either a caption or, if it is to go with a story, identify who is in the photograph and what is happening. It can be as simple as one sentence but should be complete enough to tell the reason why the photograph was taken. Identify the people in each shot by name and position, as well as the name of the organization, the event, its location, and the date it occurred.

— Never write on the back of a picture. The pressure of a pen or even a pencil will make marks on the front of the photograph. Type a separate piece of paper, cut it out, and tape it to the back of the photo with as little tape as possible.

Slides: A single slide, or a series of two to four slides, can be used on television or shown before a movie. A striking action visual in color, followed by a clearly lettered informational slide giving time, place, and date of the event is very effective. Slides can be mounted in metal1 plastic, or cardboard. Use only the very highest quality photographs for slides. This may be the "first point of contact" with your audience and you want them to know you are running a professional and competent operation.

Slide shows are good for:

— Communicating a specific idea or impression to your audience.

— Communicating a subject that is "visual," where words will not convey information effectively.

— An audience in a specific location and at a specific event.

Slides are not good for:

— Imparting a great deal of information that needs to be referred to often. Use a booklet instead.

— A short lived event (slide shows can be expensive).

— Showing where there may not be appropriate equipment for viewing available.

— A lengthy subject. Slide shows should not run more than 15-20 minutes.

Planning your slide presentation

— Define the objective of the slide show.

— Analyze the audience to which it will be shown; your message should be directed to them.

Preparing the presentation:

— Write the Script: Write the script first rather than writing around your slides. By writing your script first, you can keep the thrust of your show sharp and the pacing just the way you want it.

— Plan the Slides: To keep the show from drifting, vary the space between slide changes and their location in the sentence. Do not have every slide change done when a sentence ends, when a sentence begins, or in the middle of a sentence.

— It is not necessary to have a new slide for every new sentence. Make sure, however, that you never have more than one new thought or idea for each slide. Use as many slides as necessary to develop that thought, but never so many that the pace of the show stalls. Be creative about your slides. Make sure the slides are professional in quality and distinct, not blurred or weak in color.

— Time the Show: Check for pacing, for final length, and for delivery of the presentation (if there is to be an oral talk with the show).

— Handouts: When you make a slide show presentation, be sure there are materials for your audience to take with them (i.e., maps, flyers, brochures, samples, folders).

Writing the Script: Write a vivid opening segment to get your audience's attention and plan to use your most exciting slides at this time. Use short declarative sentences, action verbs, present tense, descriptive images, and conversational languages. While you can develop each new thought by using more than one sentence, try not to use more than three sentences for each thought; otherwise the pace will lag. The summation should leave your audience with an "upbeat" feeling. Divide the script into three sections: main thrust of your presentation, hard information, and summation. A description should be prepared for each slide and each sentence used numbered so that the presenter can easily be cued to each slide. Make new slides rather than trying to fit an old slide into your script and ensure each slide is compatible with the idea you are trying to get across.

Effective Customer Service

An important element of promotion that cannot be overlooked is customer service. Food and hospitality can advertise and promote its services extensively, but if there is no customer service program then promotional efforts will be in vain. Vital to the success of any MWR activity is the customer oriented attitude of employees. Customer service policies must start with the activity manager. Policies should be communicated to employees and supported by them. These policies and practices must become an integral part of the food and hospitality operation.

A key management philosophy which should be practiced in every food and hospitality program is the assumption that the customer is right unless a complaint is proven unjustified. Patrons who take the time to lodge complaints believe they have legitimate problems. Ignoring or responding negatively to complaints will result in nothing but ill will. These customers deserve prompt attention, ideally, inquiries should be responded to on the same day they are received.

Giving your customers what they want and need to make them happy pays great dividends. Happy customers tell their friends-approximately 72 percent of first-time customers come because of recommendations. Conversely, unhappy customers tell at least 10 other people.

Quick resolution of patron complaints lets patrons know they are important and also lessens the possibility of the complaint being aired to others. By being open to customer criticism, we develop an effective means to measure how we are serving our patrons. It is essential that food and hospitality build an effective customer service program. This starts with training employees on proper ways to respond to customer complaints. The wrong response to a customer's problem can create a negative effect which ripples when dissatisfied patrons spread their complaints.

Employees should be personable, have a neat appearance, a good telephone voice, patience, and a knowledge of the food and hospitality program. Above all, they must have a genuine interest in people. A dedicated, responsive, customer-oriented organization is one of the best contributions that can be made in this climate of heightened customer awareness.

Telephone Tips

(1) Answer promptly.

(2) Identify the activity and yourself when answering.

(3) Speak distinctly and pleasantly.

(4) Avoid making abrupt, trite, or misleading phrases.

(5) Give the caller a report and make an offer to help. "He stepped out for a few minutes. May I ask him to call you?"

(6) When necessary, give the caller an accurate telephone number or extension where the person may be reached.

(7) Volunteer your own assistance. "May I help you?" or "Could someone else help you?"

(8) Request the identity of a caller in a tactful manner.

(9) Explain delays. Be sure to let the caller know you are going to have to put the phone down and why.

(10) Take messages willingly. Write details on a suitable form and deliver them promptly.

(11) Transfer the call elsewhere only when the correct number is known. No one likes a "run around."

(12) Say goodbye pleasantly and hang up gently.

VISUAL MERCHANDISING STRATEGIES

Visual merchandising helps distinguish food and hospitality activities from other activities on or off base. When well planned, visual merchandising can help boost sales. It encompasses all aspects of activity services, including areas not typically considered income producers or sales related.

Merchandising helps make each patron's visit to the activity a memorable one, provides a unique atmosphere, and makes the entire facility more attractive, pleasant, and comfortable. Any area within the activity which can achieve these goals must be considered a potential merchandising area.

The following deserve particular attention with respect to merchandising efforts:

— Menus and Food

— Services

— Facilities

— Pricing of Services

— Uniforms

— Entertainment

Within each of these areas there are particular focuses of attention. Combined, the overall goal is the activity image, which is the way patrons perceive the activity and its services. Although the definition implies that image is an individual opinion, there are several ways the activity manager can present the club so that its image is consistent for all patrons.

Merchandising can influence the patron's perception of the activity (i.e., how it looks, its comforts, its friendliness). In fact, merchandising may be the single most important factor in affecting the patron's perception. The awareness of image-related areas deserves constant managerial attention.

Menus and Food

If the activity's primary purpose is to provide food and beverage, the menu and food are the most important areas where an image can be created. The entire activity perception can be affected by a poor or unimaginative menu. The areas within the menu that deserve merchandising attention are the use of colors, graphics, printing styles, cover design, menu item descriptive wording, size and shape of menu, and the actual choice of menu items.

Again, merchandising means providing distinctive qualities and special touches. The menu should be designed creatively and printed by a professional printer. The use of seasonal menus allows for merchandising through graphics and/or color schemes which depict seasonal activities. Menus also allow the activity manager to develop specialty dishes and merchandise them as such on the menu. Certain menu items can be emphasized and merchandised through descriptive wording. There are no limits to the usefulness of the menu in helping provide a distinctive and memorable food and beverage operation.

Food quality must reach the level of expectation created by the menu. The actual taste of the food will linger on longer, and have a much more lasting effect on the patrons' perception of the food service, than the menu. The two, the menu and the food, must be thought of as a team, with food quality being the more important consideration.

Although good food quality will compensate for a poor menu, a good menu will not compensate for poor food quality. The ultimate goal is a menu that complements food quality and vice versa. The importance of food quality as a merchandising tool is exemplified by the fact that word-of-mouth advertising is critical to the success of an activity's food operation. Merchandising the food operations through good quality food turns the patron who has had an enjoyable dining experience into an advertising medium.

Services: Services can be defined as any service offered to the patron, whether it be for profit or not. Services include food and beverages, party facilities, meeting rooms, recreational areas and/or equipment, entertainment, and other services such as telephones in Temporary Lodging Facility rooms, newspapers, and vending machines. As can be seen, there are countless areas within services where merchandising can be a factor. Merchandising services means emphasizing any special services, facilities and/or capabilities. A pool room, for instance, represents a multitude of possibilities for merchandising. Special "sharp shooter" nights, tournaments, trick shooter exhibitions and partner tournaments are only a few possibilities that turn an ordinary pool room into a potential profit producer.

Managers should evaluate their facilities in respect to potential services merchandising. Other areas which deserve consideration are recreational activities (pinball, ping pong, tennis, golf), food and beverage service (specialty ethnic nights, family nights, "all you can eat" nights), and entertainment (concerts, talent shows, dancing exhibitions, dinner shows). The key point is that there are endless ways in which activity services can be merchandised. The following steps are important in merchandising services.

— Determine exactly what services are available.

— Determine what types of services can be made available with or without capital expenditures.

— Establish a priority list of services which should be merchandised based upon market questionnaires, intuition, and informal patron surveys.

— Develop a list for each service or promotions and events which can be implemented and specially merchandised. Be sure to make them realistic and affordable.

— Establish a rough plan as to when these types of services can be offered.

Facilities

The actual condition of the activity facility is one area that is not an income producer but is, nonetheless, an area that deserves merchandising attention. A very clean, well-organized, and appealing facility will most definitely affect the patron's perception of the activity as a whole. Therefore, as previously emphasized, facilities are included in areas affecting image and should be treated as areas requiring merchandising efforts.

Some of the areas that require attention are the exterior grounds, landscape, entrance ways, hallways, carpeting, furniture, decorations, and meeting rooms. In addition, food and beverage facilities (dining rooms, bars), recreational areas, and entertainment facilities all require the same focus.

Examples of the type of merchandising that helps promote services are well-landscaped and well-maintained lawns, gardens, shrubbery, and sidewalk areas; clean and well-painted entrance ways, awnings and doors; and well-maintained carpets, woodwork, lighting fixtures, and hallway furniture. The patron who arrives at the facility and notices a well-kept and well-structured garden is seeing a merchandising effort aimed at providing appealing and attractive facilities. Conversely, an improperly maintained garden or entrance way does not help to create a favorable image.

Another example of the facility's role in merchandising is the maintenance of meeting and special function rooms. These rooms should be attractive, well-decorated and clean. The patrons using the rooms will feel more comfortable in a well-maintained meeting room and will notice the efforts to personalize the room for their functions, such as providing special decorations for weddings and parties. Again, this all helps create an overall favorable image for the activity.

Pricing of Services

Pricing is not considered a typical merchandising tool. Its primary objective is to provide income. It must be assumed, however, that the patron views pricing as a very important aspect of services. Value is the key. Providing value becomes a marketing/merchandising effort. Throughout the private sector, value is a very strongly emphasized quality in advertising and merchandising programs. The nature of pricing and services has been discussed in other sections of this manual with the emphasis placed on the fact prices are established only after critical review of:

— Cost of the service

— Profit objective

— Anticipated popularity of the service

— Competitors' prices for similar services

— Market flexibility

Fixed prices, (room rates, menu prices, drink prices) are not as amenable to merchandising considerations as are special events and promotions. Special entertainment such as concerts and various types of exhibitions, special dinner nights, and holiday parties present opportunities for price merchandising.

Special pricing could include "dinner for two," reduced prices at Happy Hours, special family rate for families attending activities, and half-price admissions to special events such as Halloween parties, Christmas balls, and St. Patrick's Day events with prizes for best costumes, the best dancers, or the "most Irish looking" participants. The low price and "all you can eat" promotion has become a prime example of how pricing and merchandising work together to produce both value and sales.

Uniforms

It is necessary to mention uniforms as a merchandising tool because they are considered a basic part of an activity's "ambiance." A well-dressed employee is one of the best merchandising tools we have. An entire staff of well-dressed employees is the ultimate goal. Uniforms, like landscaping, provide an immediate visual experience to the patron. Poorly organized and unkempt uniforms create an unfavorable image of the activity as a whole, even though they are not considered income producers or services. Uniforms should be provided to all employees, or a standard uniform should be established so that all employees may purchase similar attire. Whenever possible, uniforms should reflect the central theme of the facility. This is another way by which distinctiveness and image are created.

Entertainment

Of all the areas mentioned in this section, entertainment is the one which continually utilizes merchandising as a primary sales tool. Merchandising efforts should concentrate on personal selling, advertising, and the actual choice of entertainment. Obviously, the more familiar or more popular the entertainment, the more distinctive the activity becomes. Entertainment should always be viewed as a special activity deserving special promotional considerations.

Entertainment needs merchandising efforts to stimulate interest. It is self-defeating to offer the same kind of entertainment over and over again-its special qualities become lost. This may not be the case for very popular entertainment such as a special band that always draws big crowds, but generally, too much repetition of one form of entertainment nullifies the merchandising aspects of the event.

Some merchandising-type tools which are used for promoting entertainment are phrases such as "appearing for the first time ever," "back by popular demand," "all the way from (name of place)," and "command performance." Each of these phrases, and similar phrases, are attempts to emphasize uniqueness and distinctiveness. There can be no substitute for merchandising; it offers an opportunity for the activity to impress patrons with its attention to details. Perhaps the most important outgrowth of good merchandising, however, is that not only do patrons benefit from management's commitment to provide special touches, but the activity also benefits from increased patron participation.

Marketing Plan

Planning is essential to the success of any business. The marketing planning process attempts to organize thinking about the future, what must be accomplished, and when it must be done. Since most management problems happen on a day-to-day basis, most managers focus only on the present. Long-range planning to these managers is next week.

An effective planning process is to your best advantage. A marketing plan will provide you with a blueprint for making important business decisions. The process requires a thorough evaluation of your activity, and upon completion you will have outlined your business's specific goals, strategies, programs, and budget. This will provide a rational, logical sense of direction for your activity and detail your strategy for success. Among the benefits to be realized are: A sense of direction that is rational and logical.

— Coordinated effort and maximized use of resources.

— Indexes to measure and evaluate how the organization is doing.

— Improved public relations allowing better interpretation of the organization's goals and achievements.

— Increased employee involvement.

— Improved staff capabilities to manage and assess overall program operations.

— Increased foresight in terms of meeting future community needs and operation requirements, thereby reducing crisis management.

Although the Food and Hospitality Director and the activity level manager can tell you what they would like to do, often nothing is written-no objectives, no tasking, no milestone dates. As a result, many activities are at a level of stagnation, with no visible improvements patrons can relate to, no lessons learned for improvement, and in some instances, no new equipment for improving the activities.

Some of the most common statements from managers who do not prepare written plans are:

— Business techniques cannot be used in nonprofit organizations.

— Day-to-day crises need attention, leaving little time for planning.

— Efforts that require thinking about the future are difficult and uncertain.

— Managers have never been trained in the planning process.

Planning is both strategic and operational. This section focuses on strategic planning which is primarily concerned with long-range issues, such as the mix of products within a product portfolio. A mix of products in different stages of the life cycle is also an aspect of strategic planning. Diversifying a menu would be an example of this. "Fad" items will generate substantial profits, but have a limited life cycle compared to more stable items. An example would be a popular appetizer item as compared to the ever-popular cheeseburger. The marketing planning process requires you to consider the wants and needs of your customers, or that the process be market driven. In researching and developing your plan, your experience and customers will be invaluable resources. Other suggested personnel to consult include your:

— MWR Marketing Personnel

— Installation Commander

— Installation Sergeant Major

— Base Master Planner

— Other Food and Hospitality Activity Managers

The following are important principles to consider when developing a marketing plan.

— The process of planning should be done by outlining your steps before beginning the process.

— Relevant planning involves fact finding and analysis.

— Planning is a continuous process and the primary responsibility of management.

— Planning is more than a staff process and requires obtaining input from your customers and other food and hospitality managers, and taking into account your competition and experience.

— Groups and/or individuals who are directly affected by planning decisions should have the opportunity to influence these decisions at appropriate points during the planning process.

— Persons accountable for implementing plans should be involved in the planning.

— Related tasks should be grouped to determine if they will support a common objective.

— Tasks should be clear and accurate.

To develop a marketing plan, you must:

1. Examine your current marketing situation.
    a. Identify trends and examine your local environment.
    b. Examine potential opportunities and threats to your program.
    c. Determine the strengths and weaknesses of your program.
    d. Ask yourself: "What business am I in?"
    e. Identify who your patrons are and what they need.
2. Set objectives and goals for your marketing plan.
3. Determine the best marketing strategy.
    a. Determine target markets.
    b. Develop the best marketing mix.
    c. Complete a competitive analysis.
4. Develop a plan of action.
5. Determine a budget and set controls.
6. Develop an Executive Summary.

Step 1. Examine your current marketing situation

a.Identify trends and examine your local environment

A marketing plan must include an analysis of your local environment, industry trends, economic indicators, and political and social changes relevant to your products or services. Your program is affected by these factors, and you must be knowledgeable to ensure your program changes as required by the changing environment in which you operate. Your local environment consists of your specific activity's components plus other on-base elements, such as the Marine Corps Exchange, Base Security, and the different ranks of Marines. Your activity's components consist of:

— Personnel (yourself, supervisors, staff, maintenance, etc.)

— Facilities (dining rooms, sleeping rooms, cafeterias, cocktail lounges, entertainment rooms, kitchens, etc.)

— Supplies and equipment (tables, chairs, food preparation equipment, etc.)

— Other food service facilities, both on and off base (i.e., McDonalds, Holiday Inn, convenience stores)

Industry trends must be closely observed. For instance, an increase in health and fitness awareness causes an increased demand for diet or health foods and beverages. Such a trend may lead to: smaller entree portions; less fried foods, more broiled and steamed; less fatty meats and desserts and more vegetables and fruits; less white bread and more whole-grain breads; less heavy, "gravy-type" foods and greater demand for foods lower in saturated fats and cholesterol; or more salads, soups, and appetizers.

To interpret trends, compare leading economic indicators, such as unemployment, inflation, federal budget cuts, and an increase in unemployment. What do the relationships between these indicators mean to you? In general, if leading economic indicators are positive, such as an increase in employment, the market potential for most goods or services will increase. For example, there may be greater demand for the more expensive items on your menu.

Conversely, demand for the more economical choices may increase as economic conditions worsen. All economic indicators should be viewed solely as one piece of evidence in determining the strategies to be incorporated into your marketing plan. Use these indicators to assist you in your planning. Unforeseen political, social, and economic events may cause the economic indicator to become invalid in a short period of time. For this reason indicators should not be used as "absolutes."

Political and social changes will also affect your current marketing strategy. Primary sources for political and social changes are the newspaper (local, regional, and national), television, and radio. This is particularly evident in third world countries where revolutions, riots, and other social-political disturbances often threaten marketing activities.

In the United States at the national level, political actions such as deregulation, increased taxes, and the elimination of trade barriers can have profound effects on marketing activities. Sometimes a change in the political party in control can affect marketing plans. At the state level, political factors such as the acceptance or rejection of bond issues and urban renovation, can have positive or negative marketing implications.

Social changes, such as trends toward conservative or liberal life styles, have both immediate and long-term marketing implications. Changes in mobility, marriage and divorce, working women, and many other societal factors may be considered in the preparation of a marketing plan. Since each marketing plan must be custom-made, only those factors which have direct influence on your products should be included.

When identifying trends, concentrate on those which affect your specific food and hospitality activity. You must observe the factors over a period of time to determine if it is in fact a trend and not just a fad. Also, compare the relationship between leading indicators, such as unemployment and inflation, and determine what the relationship means to your activity. Use the newspaper, both local and national, television, and radio as primary sources of information. Your success will depend on how current and updated you are on what is occurring within your geographical area.

The following are examples of the types of trends which could affect your business.

— *Local Installation Environment*

  — Command emphasis on reasonably priced entertainment for young, enlisted Marines.

  — Mission changes because of deployments.

  — Generally old, run-down appearance of facilities.

  — Skilled personnel near the installation.

  — Large pool of possible clientele, such as young adults (20's-30's) with children.

— *Local Area Trends*

  — "Happy Hour" specials.

  — Free hors d'oeuvres during select times.

— Diversified ethnic foods, such as Mexican or Vietnamese entrees.

— Carry-out or delivery service.

— Military discounts frequently offered off base.

— *Economic Indicators*

— Increase in unemployment.

— Inflation rate.

— Budget cuts.

— *Industry Trends*

— Offering of "light" foods.

— More and greater variety food bars.

— Offering of ethnic food items.

— Frequent stay programs.

— Weekend getaway packages offered.

— *Marine-Corps Trends*

— Decrease in alcohol consumption.

— Increase in variety and demand for appetizers.

— Increased interest in casual dining with a theme such as Mexican, Italian, etc.

— Greater demand for seafood and poultry.

— *Political and Social Changes*

— Deregulation.

— Tax increases.

— Mobility.

— Marriage rates.

— Average family size.

— Aging society.

b. Examine potential opportunities and threats to your program.

As you examine your current marketing situation, you must examine potential opportunities and threats to your program. Opportunities are areas where you enjoy a competitive advantage over your competition due to the local environment factors previously listed. Threats are situations that might have an unfavorable effect on your program if no marketing action is taken. Sometimes, threats can become opportunities by diverting resources to another program that better meets the needs of your patrons.

Examine the opportunities and threats to your program and decide what to do to enhance your opportunities and minimize your threats. This will help you develop your marketing goals and objectives.

Examples of opportunities and threats follow as do characteristics of successful food and hospitality activities. Some examples are:

— *Opportunities*

— Location is convenient for patrons.

— Cuisine and menu based on healthful foods and overall "wellness."

— A menu emphasizing seafood, naturally prepared foods, and fresh produce (for an installation located in an area that has these items in ready supply).

— A Chinese or other food menu for lunch service as an alternative to the "fast food" readily available.

— *Threats*

— Budget pressures, cut-backs, and reduced appropriated funding support of programs.

— Local military mission changes may result in a decreased patron base.

— Increasing focus on alcohol abuse programs and drunken driving may further reduce bar business and erode high margin sales.

— Fast food restaurant coming on base may erode sales, especially lunch sales.

— Convenience store coming on base may cause a decline in food sales.

Before identifying your activities's opportunities and threats, consider the following general concepts for each market segment.

— *Characteristics of a Successful Enlisted Club*

— Good, convenient location near single Marine housing (within walking distance).

— Good entertainment program with a DJ and dance floor.

— Attractive, clean decor and adequate size (i.e., one seat for each 7.3 persons living on base).

— Good drinks, service, and snack food.

— Competitive prices to off-base bars.

— Opposite gender patronizes the club.

— Marines and civilians under 21 years of age can use the club, but can not be served alcoholic beverages.

— Good size and fully equipped game room.

— Adequate operating hours.

— *Characteristics of a Successful SNCO Club*

— Attracts Department of Defense civilians with location near work/office areas of all eligible patrons for lunch business.

— Location on main roadway near main gate.

— Active group of eligible retirees.

— Location near recreation/fitness facilities or same included in club.

— Good product/service mix of food and beverages at prices competitive to off-base facilities.

— Good entertainment program.

— Good size and fully equipped game room.

— Adequate parking.

— Adequate operating hours.

— Good bingo program.

— Attractive, clean decor and adequate size.

— Good catering/sales program and adequate banquet space.

— Dining room suitable for family usage.

– *Characteristics of a Successful Officers' Club*

— Majority of junior officers living on base.

— Attracts Department of Defense civilians with location near work/office areas of all eligible patrons for lunch business.

— A large active group of eligible retirees with base security passes allowing evening access.

— Location on main roadway near main gate for ease of off-base access.

— Location near recreation/fitness facilities or same included in club.

— Good product/service mix of food and beverage.

— Prices competitive to off-base restaurants.

— Good entertainment program for all groups.

— Commanding officer setting an example of club usage and membership.

— Good size and fully equipped game room.

— Alcoholic (deglamorization) policy not overly restrictive.

— Good membership dues program.

— Adequate parking.

— Full range of operating hours.

— Attractive decor and adequate size.

— Good catering sales program and adequate banquet space.

— Dining room suitable for family usage.

— *Characteristics of a Successful Fast Service/Snack Bar*

— Located near major activity.

— Attractive decor and adequate size.

— Good product/service mix of food and beverage at competitive prices.

— Operating hours which compliment the major activities nearby.

— Fast service and/or possible delivery.

— Located near on-base housing.

— Suitable for family usage.

— *Characteristics of a Successful Temporary Lodge Facility*

— High occupancy factor

— Clean, comfortable and well appointed rooms

— Adequate operating hours

— Good customer feedback system

c. Determine the strengths and weaknesses of your program.

There are two types of strengths and weaknesses-"known" and "unknown". Strengths and weaknesses as seen by your patrons are known strengths and weaknesses. Patron surveys and "word-of-mouth" are good sources to discover your known strengths and weaknesses. You will obtain information on customer satisfaction such as how your customers view the quality of your facility, equipment, personnel, and whether their needs are being met. Suggestion boxes, comments, and surveys will identify your patrons' views on your operation's strengths and weaknesses.

Your patrons may not be aware of some additional strengths and weaknesses in your program. Your familiarity with your day-to-day suppliers and equipment, personnel capabilities or problems, or other factors that can influence your program, are examples of unknown strengths and weaknesses. Information gained from yourself and your personnel is useful in determining the unknown strengths and weaknesses of your operation.

Examples:

— *Known strengths*

 — Marine Corps costs and prices are lower than private competition.

 — The installation has a substantial location advantage for patrons living on the base and for those working on the base during day time hours.

 — The quality of food at the clubs on base, its preparation and cooking, get consistently high marks from patrons.

 — Hours of operation that suit the patrons' needs.

— *Known weaknesses*

 — The clubs on base have a poor reputation among patrons for atmosphere, especially for family dining.

 — Parking is inadequate on weekends.

 — Restroom plumbing in serious need of repair.

 — The cleanliness of the facility is lacking.

 — A reputation for poor service.

— *Unknown strengths*

 — On base profits of clubs and snackbars are high, although the margin is very thin.

 — Mechanisms have been established (comment cards and patron surveys) for patron evaluation and feedback on a daily basis.

— The base has strong command support for funding requests to improve the food and hospitality activities.

— *Unknown weaknesses*

— Promotional efforts are limited and inconsistent.

— Staff morale is low, and employee turnover is high.

— Reduced price promotions cannot be used freely because of the need to meet profit goals more from food sales and less from alcohol sales.

— You do not receive strong management and command support for innovative new projects you wish to implement.

d. Ask yourself: "What business am I in?"

You have looked at trends, your local environment, opportunities and threats, and strengths and weaknesses. Now you need to ask, "What is our reason for existing?" You need a clear statement of purpose so everyone involved in delivering your program can focus their efforts on that purpose. A statement of purpose will help both management and staff conduct their programming efforts in a common direction.

A statement of business purpose identifies what you do in the broadest terms. It also helps you to identify with those whom you are serving- your patrons. As these examples show, your business purpose should focus on what benefits your programs offer to patrons and how your program is distinctly different from other establishments.

Examples:

— Providing social and recreational facilities, food service, and refreshments to commissioned officers and their families.

— Providing a convenient place for the Master Sergeant to escape the pressures of work and to socialize in a relaxed atmosphere.

— Providing complete banquet and catering services including event planning, menu planning, food preparation, food and beverage set-up and service, table settings and glassware, facilities and facility decorating, and after event clean-up.

— Providing the enlisted Marine Corps member with quality food and contemporary entertainment with an emphasis on service.

— Providing convenient fast food to MWR patrons.

— Providing a family oriented atmosphere, catering to patrons with children.

— Providing affordable lodging on mainside, plus mountain chalets for recreational retreats.

e. Identify who your patrons are and what they need and want.

Identify your patrons in basic terms of gender, rank, and marital status. You should also identify, as closely as possible1 common interests or characteristics of your patron population. For example, determine your patrons family size and how they spend their leisure time. From these characteristics of patron participation you can develop your programs.

The best way to identify your patrons' needs and desires is through marketing research, which is discussed in detail beginning on page six of this NAVMC. Research results can provide a major stepping stone for meeting market needs. As market needs and wants constantly change with market conditions, so must your surveys. In times of recession and inflation, for instance, value becomes increasingly important. Lower prices (consistent with profit objectives) and less expensive programs, become more important. As expendable income increases, more services, better quality food, and top quality programs may be stressed. Marketing research serves a purpose to food and hospitality activities by forging a formal bond between patron needs and activity offerings. The more often the two coincide, the more successful the activity is in the eyes of both parties. Before identifying your patron profile, consider the following general concepts for each market segment.

Enlisted

— *E1-E3*
  - — mostly single
  - — wants to meet opposite sex
  - — wants lively, current entertainment
  - — enjoys alcoholic beverages (though may be under 21)
  - — wants informal, non-military atmosphere
  - — eats fast food
  - — many Privately Owned Vehicles (POV's)

— *E4-E5*
  - — many are married
  - — enjoys program that appeals to spouse
  - — many live off base
  - — limited disposable income due to family size
  - — desires family dining

SNCOs

— *E6-E9*

- — older, career oriented Marine Corps personnel
- — close knit, almost fraternal group
- — club use builds esprit de corps
- — desires family dining
- — party/banquet usage important
- — many live off base
- — reduced MWR activity evening use after leaving base

Officers

— *01-03*

- — many are single
- — wants to meet opposite sex
- — good surplus income for singles
- — many POV's
- — wants informal, non-military atmosphere
- — married officers desire family dining

— *04-010*

- — many are married
- — activity must appeal to spouse
- — mostly use club for lunch
- — official functions important
- — like more formal atmosphere
- — like more reserved entertainment
- — family life reduces disposable income

Step 2. Set objectives and goals for your marketing plan

You are now ready to define marketing goals and objectives for your program. Marketing goals (strategies) identify what you are going to do in broad terms. Marketing objectives are specific means to achieve your goals. They state what will be done, when it will be done, and how the result will be measured. When writing your goals and objectives, consider the preceding steps you have just completed. You have:

a) Identified trends affecting your operation and examined the local environment influencing your activity.

b) Examined potential opportunities and threats to your program.

c) Determined strengths and weaknesses of your program (both known and unknown).

d) Specified your business purpose so you can focus your efforts.

e) Identified your patrons and their needs.

As you establish your marketing goals and objectives, address these items. Your goals and objectives should stress strengths and minimize weaknesses, reflect your business purpose, and satisfy your patrons' current and potential needs.

Examples

Goal: Establish a healthy cuisine program with existing facilities, equipment and staff to meet the needs of MWR patrons.

Objectives:

— Establish cuisine and menu by January 31 at a cost not to exceed $200.

— Initiate promotional campaign by September 20 using a mix of all available print and audio-visual media.

— Consider discount pricing (two for one) or promotional "give-aways" to increase numbers of patrons by 10 percent within six months of program initiation.

Goal: Improve the image of the activity in order to increase family patronage.

Objectives:

— Train staff by October 10 how to handle rowdy or disruptive patrons.

— Institute changes in menu based on patron surveys by October 30.

— Promote new "family" program using indoctrination sessions, through base newsletters, direct mail, wives' club, and word-of-

— mouth.

Step 3: Determine the best marketing strategy

Marketing strategy is the fundamental marketing logic by which the business unit intends to achieve its marketing objectives. Marketing strategy consists of a coordinated set of decisions on (a) target markets, (b) marketing mix, and (c) marketing expenditure level. Marketing strategy is the "game plan" by which you hope to "win." The three components of a marketing strategy are target markets, the best marketing mix, and competitive analysis.

a. Determine your target market.

A sound marketing strategy calls for giving different degrees of emphasis to the various market segments making up the population. These segments differ in their preferences, responses to marketing effort, and profitability. They differ in the degree to which an activity is able to produce satisfaction. Instead of going after all the market segments with equal fervor, you are smart to allocate your effort and energy to those market segments you can serve best; these segments are your target market.

Your population is defined as all active duty and retired military, reservists, their family members, and other eligible patrons, such as civilians who work on base. Your target market will depend on your type of activity. If you are the Junior Enlisted Club Manager, obviously your primary target market is the E1 - E5 market segment. You can develop your target market definition further, however, by considering what other population segments you serve. Who else frequently uses your facility? Do civilians for lunch, wives clubs for afternoon meetings, junior officer's for "wetting downs"? Whose needs can you best meet?

b. Develop the best marketing mix.

The services and programs your activity offers are among the many offered at your installation. Some services and programs seem to go on forever; some last for just a short time. Some start strongly and then fade quickly; some start weakly and seem to get stronger with age. What are the factors that cause these differences? Can you predict, in advance, how your program will behave? Is there a "life cycle" for programs?

The answer is yes, although there is no single life cycle for each and every program, and not all programs go through every stage of the life cycle in the same way. From the initiation of a new program idea to the completion of the program, however, there are various steps. The program life cycle consists of four stages.

Stage I - Introduction: This is when a program idea is first considered for implementation. At this time, there should be extensive promotion of the activity to ensure initial participation. During this period a program's quality and patron satisfaction are top priority. Although the techniques shown below are considered essential throughout a program's life cycle, they are especially important during the introduction stage.

(1) Establish a competitive advantage.

(2) Position the program clearly. Emphasize rewards and end user benefits, such as enjoyment and relaxation.

(3) Use the new program/concept name repetitively for reinforcement via copy, theme, story line, logos, jingles, etc.

(4) Project a distinctive, individualistic personality and image.

(5) Keep the message simple.

(6) Generate consumer identification-target market.

Stage II - Take Off: At this point most usage will come via word-of-mouth. It is extremely important that the quality, service, and value of the program be at its highest. Future growth stems directly from this period.

Stage III - Mature Stage: At this point, the activity has its highest number of participants, but may not continue to grow. Questions that need to be asked of management, staff, and consumers are:

— Is there a new way to offer the services? Is there a new way to use it as is? Are there other uses if modified?

— Can it be adapted? What else is like this? What other ideas does this suggest? What could we copy?

— Can it be modified? Given a new twist? Changed in color, meaning, motion, sound, odor, form, and shape? Are other changes possible?

— Can it be magnified? What should be added? More time? Greater frequency? Stronger? Higher? Longer? Shorter? Lighter? Omit something? Streamline? Split up?

— What can we substitute? Other ingredients? Other processes?

— Rearrange? Interchange components? Other patterns? Other layout? Transpose cause and effect? Change the pace? Change the schedule?

— Reverse it? Transpose positive and negative? Turn it backwards? Upside down? Reverse roles?

— Combine it? How about a blend? An assortment? An ensemble? Purposes?

Stage IV - Decline: This is the stage where it is important to decide whether to continue the program. If patrons aren't participating and a number of promotions have been tried, it may be in the best interest of the command to stop the program. Why waste valuable resources, such as money, time, and personnel for a program that serves so few.

As you analyze your programs' life cycle, asking these questions may help place your programs in their proper stage of the life cycle, and choose the appropriate overall approach to marketing those programs. Is your program old and established or new and unknown? If you offer an established program, you are faced with a "positioning" challenge. You must position your program in a way that distinguishes it from your competition. A new program has its own natural position.

Is your program a long or short-lived program? An example of a long-term program would be Sunday brunch because it has "staying power" and will go on indefinitely. "Cajun" cooking is an example of a short-lived program which is not expected to go on indefinitely. Is your program staying current? If your program areas and programming techniques or technology are changing, and you are not, you can count on losing some of your share of the market. Who is your competition? Do you have one competitor or many? What is the likelihood of your having more competition in the future? Are you doing something to protect your position? Is everybody getting into the act? If so, your program may be maturing and your share of the market will decrease.

Is the market or target population growing or declining? In the food and hospitality businesses at large, the market has been growing. How is the Marine Corps installation you are serving doing? If your installation is losing or gaining operational units or tenant commands/activities, you will see a corresponding decrease or increase in participation.

c. Complete competitive analysis

A knowledge of competitors is critical in designing effective marketing strategies. It is important to understand what the competition is doing even if you believe they are wrong. This does not imply that spy-like activities are needed, nor that a disproportionate amount of time should be spent investigating or worrying about the competitor.

The bulk of information needed about your competitors is normally available if you keep your business eyes and ears open and train members of your staff to do likewise. Several common sources of information about competitors follow.

— *Newspaper Articles*

— *Company Literature.* Available through sales information, franchise information, advertisements, public information releases, and other company publications.

— *Individuals.* Salespeople who call on competitors. Individuals who have recently left the employment of a competitor. Individuals you are interviewing who have experience in the field.

— *Observation.* By occasionally visiting your competitors' facilities, by acting as a prospective customer and by purchasing the products of your competitor (this can be fun.)

— *The Competitor.* Talk to your competitors. People like to talk about themselves and what their business is doing even though they know they are talking with a competitor.

— Other Employees.

— *Friends and Relatives.* Word-of-mouth is the best method. Talk to people who have been in contact with your competitors and will share information with you about their experiences. This usually consists of complaints or compliments about your competitor's product/service.

Terms to Help You Analyze and Use Competitive Information

— *Trends.* A temporary price decrease by a competitor may mean little. A trend of consistently lowering prices could be very meaningful. For instance, it could indicate the operation is systematically lowering prices to gain market share and achieve greater chunks of the market. Consistently: lower prices could also mean the company is in deep trouble. Look for trends and seriously question what they mean.

— *Variances.* Variances from normal procedures often indicate a troubled competitor. They may also be signs of test markets or new strategies.

— *Consistency.* Consistency in marketing strategies is normally verified by trends that are long-run in nature and relatively free of deviations.

— *Shakeups in Management.* Major shakeups in management are commonly followed by changes in policies and strategies. Watch for large-scale shakeups in management and anticipate change.

— *Financial Changes.* A decline in earnings and poor financial ratios often precede changes in marketing strategies. Changes are most likely when negative or undesirable financial results have occurred.

— *Sudden and New Success.* The "new kid on the block" is often the most dangerous. It is often tempting to dismiss a new competitor as a "flash in the pan" and overlook the fact that the customer is buying more from this new competitor than from you. You should logically and objectively examine your new competition and then decide how to counteract it.

Step 4: Develop a plan of action

In the military, a plan of action (POA) is accomplished by using a mix of personnel, material, weapons, and their placement. In marketing terms, a POA is accomplished by using a mix of program, price, promotion, and service delivery. Your POA should be centered around a program which allows your patrons the opportunity to satisfy their needs and wants. Your program can be a service, activity, facility, place, or idea.

Think of your program the way your patrons do. The physical elements of your program should be considered. These elements include the setting, quality and condition of your facilities, grounds, equipment, food, and entertainment. Do your patrons not participate in some programs because they do not like the atmosphere? Your management and staff are also part of your program. What do your patrons think of them? Does management and staff regularly talk to your patrons face-to-face? Are promises to patrons always kept, even if it means overtime?

You should consider variations in your program format. Some example variations would be: open dining, special events, special interest group functions, different types of services and menus. There may be new or different ways in which you can mix program participants, physical settings, relationships, and interactions among participants, to hold the interest of current patrons or attract new patrons.

To develop a POA, you must first define the program you intend to offer. It may be a new program, based on customer demand, or a revision to a current program. Next determine a timeline, the required budget, price to charge patrons, and how it will be promoted. The price you establish for your program depends on a number of factors:

— What your patrons are willing to pay for the benefits they receive (how many will you attract or turn away at any given price for the level of benefits you provide to your patrons?)

— What your overall pricing philosophy is (do you have a policy of free dessert or non-alcoholic beverage for designated drivers?)

— Your financial performance and profit goals (do you want to make money or break even?)

Patrons at different pay grades may have different amounts of disposable income to spend on your programs. As the perceived value of your programs increase so can price, to an extent, without loss of patrons. Revenues per patron may increase as price increases, but at some level of price, no patron may choose to participate. This is an example of the demand for your programs and services not being infinitely elastic to price. An additional pricing idea is using discount pricing or "give-aways"- price promotions-to introduce your program. Discounts may cut revenues, but will stimulate demand and create awareness of your program. Choose a pricing approach to best suit your needs.

Managers should use a combination of historical participation trends and educated estimates when considering the potential success of various marketing promotions. The two key considerations are:

— the price charged for an event, and

— the estimation of attendance figures.

The price charged for an event or promotion should follow the same guidelines as for all other activity pricing (cost, profit, competition, market flexibility, popularity) and should also contain a contingency for cost increases.

Attendance may fluctuate as to the time of the year, the weather, and the base occupancy. This too must be taken into account in all estimations.

Promotional efforts are most effective when a mix of tools is used. You have already determined the target audience for your program and your market position for each of these groups. You need to select the best promotional tools to reach these audiences.

You may have several programs or activities which are part of your marketing plan For example, if you are the manager of a Club, you may have plans for bingo, Sunday brunch, Wednesday night DJ, etc. If this is your situation, you will want to take a final look at the marketing strategies you developed for each of your separate programs. Make sure that your marketing POA reflects the proper mix of program, price, and promotion elements.

Step 5: Determine a budget and set controls

Determining Your Budget

Your goals, strategies, and plan of action will help you formulate a supporting budget statement for your activity. The budget statement is essentially a projected profit and loss statement. On the revenue side, it shows the forecast number of units that would be sold and the average net profit. On the expense side, it shows the costs of production, physical distribution, and marketing, broken down into finer categories. The difference, or projected profit, is shown. Management reviews your budget, and once approved, the budget is the basis for material procurement, production scheduling, manpower planning, and marketing operations. You need to measure your progress toward achieving your marketing objectives. Progress should be measured at several levels along the way.

You will also have to make a decision on the dollar level of marketing expenditures. Even with an optimal marketing mix, a company may be spending too much or too little on marketing. Companies typically establish their marketing budget at some conventional percentage of the sales goal. Companies entering a new market have to spend a fairly high amount of marketing dollars in relation to anticipated sales in the hope of building their market share. Companies know that the more they spend on marketing, the higher their sales will be. They need to know their break-even point where sales equal costs, leaving a zero profit margin.

When formulating your marketing budget, give thought to the anticipated income and expenses of all marketing promotions and events planned for the year. Keep in mind that marketing is a continuous process. Marketing plans and promotions include not only the events themselves, but also the costs associated with ongoing marketing functions such as direct mail, research efforts, and other administrative costs associated with such activities. Consider the following as you develop your marketing budget:

1. All proposals for marketing program expenditures should be required to show profit objectives before being included in the overall budget.

2. All proposals should contain supportive data on cost and revenue forecasts. The forecasts indicate from where supportive data was retrieved and where fluctuations can be anticipated.

3. The marketing budget should be reviewed on a quarterly basis so that progress and/or revisions can be made. Food and hospitality managers should

review their marketing budget at the completion of each special promotion so that there is immediate feedback on forecasted versus actual figures.

4. All budgeting should be flexible enough to allow for tactical moves, if necessary. There may be times when a particular marketing promotion could use an extra "injection" of advertising dollars to promote sales. The budget should allow for this contingency.

Since managers are being asked to predict their marketing efforts over the course of a year, some review must be built into the budget. For instance, an entertainer may cancel an engagement and unless an adjustment is made, the anticipated profit will not be realized. This type of review should be planned quarterly.

Setting Controls

First, you need to know if you are accomplishing your objectives within budget. At least once a month you should compare your progress with your projected objectives. You should monitor your progress, concentrating on the exceptions to your plan. Consider both good and bad exceptions for example, whether you are behind schedule, or under budget. The actions you take to deal with the exceptions should be written down.

After you measure your results, the success of your efforts will need to be determined. Some examples of measures of success are shown below. Review these, and then develop your own. Ask yourself, "How will I know if I have accomplished my goal and how will I ensure that my marketing efforts will enable me to maintain the program at a successful level?"

Measures Of Success

— Number of new faces gathering in your facility during the month.

— Patron satisfaction level from survey of patrons, such as 85 percent of patrons rate program t1satisfactory" or better.

— Cost recovery of 60 percent compared with margin set in program objective.

— Number of patrons who enjoy special programs such as Happy Hour or Mexican entrees on the menu.

Step 6: Develop an Executive Summary

Your marketing plan should open with a short summary of the main goals and recommendations to be presented in the plan. The Executive Summary permits higher management to quickly grasp the main thrust of each plan and then read further in search of the information that is most critical in evaluating the plan. To facilitate this, a table of contents should follow the Executive Summary which is always the first printed sheet in your document.

2

Service Quality Management

Delivering quality service is one of the major challenges facing hospitality managers in the opening years of the next millennium. It is an essential condition for success in the emerging, keenly competitive, global hospitality markets. While the future importance of delivering quality hospitality service is easy to discern and to agree on, doing so presents some difficult and intriguing management issues.

Since the delivery of hospitality service always involves people, these issues center on the management of people, and in particular on the interactions between guests and staff, interactions that are called service encounters. In the eyes of the guests, the hospitality businesses will succeed or fail depending on the cumulative impact of the service encounters in which they have participated.

Service encounters are the building blocks of quality hospitality service. How can hospitality businesses manage them more effectively? Here we suggest a two step process in the evaluation of a service chain.

First, hospitality managers should identify each encounter in the chain that they wish to take apart, and then single out those that are of operational or strategic significance – in effect, focusing in on the few encounters that really make a difference to guest experience and thus to the bottom line.

Second, apply what we have called the 6 S's to improving these critical encounters through effective redesign.

Let's see how that would work in realistic situations.

While the first step may seem obvious, it is important to identify a service chain and then to break it down into the component encounters. Just how much detail is needed? Too much detail takes time and resources, and may confuse rather than clarify. Too little and we may miss important problems. The process is iterative, with more detail needed in some areas and less in others, and with an overriding consideration that the chain is assessed not just from the point of view of a manager but also from that of a guest.

Which are the encounters that really matter? Those that add significant value to the guest, those that cost in time or money, those that help to differentiate the business from its competitors, and those where significant innovation is possible or occurring.

Hospitality service encounters run the gamut from those that are very trivial to those that are highly critical. They vary greatly in their nature and may be simple or complex, standard or custom, low tech or high tech, remote or friendly, low or high skill, frequent or occasional, and so on. They can be instrumental dealing with the performance of necessary utilitarian activities or can involve emotion-laden hospitality events.

An initial management task is to understand a service encounter by discerning and dealing with those attributes that are most important to guests. In doing so, pertinent questions must be raised about the specific service encounter(s) under consideration. With respect to a particular service encounter, hospitality managers might raise many questions like the following:

— Exactly what happened?

— What were the guest reactions?

— Should it be done differently?

— What resources would assure optimal performance?

— What changes should be made?

— How can such changes best be put into effect?

The specific encounter(s) under consideration will, of course, indicate the kinds of questions that should be pursued. It is important to obtain adequate information to understand the situation thoroughly. Determining the context of a situation relating to a hospitality encounter that has gone wrong establishes parameters for improvement.

All this is part of the second step. With the information at hand hospitality managers can organize, and analyze the data and it is here that the 6S approach can help. These are:

— Specification

— Staff

— Space

— System

— Support
— Style

Specification means clearly detailing information about the what, when, where, and how, of service encounters. It requires giving careful thought to the linkages between particular service encounters and others in the service chain.

The starting point for hospitality service encounter analysis is specifying clearly the overall service strategy and what it is designed to achieve. Is the purpose cost or service quality leadership? Is it to provide unique service values, customized or standardized, complex or simple, frequent or occasional? Is it to provide service at any reasonable cost? Is service limited to a luxury package, or does it include budget travellers?

Which staff members are involved in providing the service? What skills do they need? What training has been provided? How committed are they to service goals? Is team cooperation or individual empowerment required? What attitudes are appropriate— friendly, open, helpful, warm service, or efficient, unobtrusive, uninvolving, unthreatening service? What staff members deal with guests? How close are the 'backroom' staff to guests? Are staff presentations and appearances appropriate?

To what extent are guests involved in the provision of service? What skill, knowledge, information, or experience do guests need to fulfill their roles? What are likely guest expectations? What communication occurred between guest and service provider? Did the dynamics of the exchange proceed smoothly? Do any language and cultural barriers exist?

Where will the service encounter occur? Is the space appropriately designed to facilitate the service encounter? Is there adequate space to handle each of the activities such as waiting, completing forms, storing or handling luggage, assembling tours? Is signage appropriate? Is the decor attractive to guests and supportive of activities that have to be carried out?

Are the necessary systems to support the encounter in place? Is the information necessary to respond effectively to guests' needs readily available? Is the appropriate technology being fully used? Are the interfaces between different functions such as housekeeping and front office, sales and front office, fully operational? What measurements of quality, or performance, are in use? Are they the most helpful for both service providers and managers? Are the criteria for success clearly defined? Is everyone involved aware of guest needs and concerns?

Are the service providers given the facilities and financial and human support needed to do the job? Is the technology appropriate? Have employees been given the training needed? Are incentive and reward systems geared to the tasks to be performed? Is supervision supportive? Does organization structure help or hinder performance?Are the suggested procedures appropriate?

How should the service encounter be conducted, given the enterprise culture? Is the management style, and marketing orientation, appropriate for the tasks? Do service providers have the appropriate attitudes? Is the right emphasis being placed on service quality?

When hospitality managers have carried out this two step process they will be in an excellent position to make decisions that will both improve the quality of hospitality services provided and guest perceptions of them. Zeroing in on hospitality service quality in this manner will help hospitality businesses meet the service challenges of the millennium, enhance their market positions, and reap the associated profit rewards.

SERVICE QUALITY AND COMPETITIVENESS

In the last few decades, business competitiveness has increasingly become a key study area as a consequence of economic globalization, increasing economic integration, and market liberalization as well as the many social, political, and economic changes that are taking place. A review of the theoretical models of business competitiveness reveals the significance of two kinds of factors in regard to this area - internal factors pertaining to the actual firm, and external factors related to the structure of the industry in which the firm operates as well as the economy of the country as a whole. Empirical evidence should corroborate these models by providing sufficient data to identify the relative significance of each individual factor regarding the global improvement of business competitiveness. However, most available studies are partial since they focus on quantifying the effects of macroeconomic variables, the effects of sector variables, or the effects of strictly business-oriented variables.

Quality of service has been one the most widely investigated factors among those strictly related to business. In this context, business competitiveness is positively related to matching the characteristics of the service to the ideal preferences of clients, i.e., their level of satisfaction. This fact reveals the key role of service quality on the improvement of business competitiveness, and how this has an effect not only outside the actual firm, but also on the variables within it. However, most relevant research on this issue deals with the theoretical study of the relationships that exist between quality and business competitiveness or with partial empirical relationships between variables. The aim of this matter is to analyze - from a global perspective - the main relationships existing between service quality and businesses competitiveness.

The data used to empirically verify this model were gathered from hotels owned by a national hotel company in Andalusia. The client survey carried out by the hotel - in the form of questionnaires - was the basis for creating the service quality indicators and establishing their most relevant dimensions. On the other hand, the economic and financial data pertaining to the hotels served to create competitiveness indicators for each of them. The results obtained were used to empirically verify a set of key hypotheses regarding the competitiveness of these hotels and to propose measures designed to improve this.

Theoretical Model

Most research dealing with the effects of quality on business competitiveness generally falls into one of two categories, depending on the kind of relationships under study. The first encompasses those works analyzing the external effects of quality on competitiveness, while the second includes those that focus on the internal effects. External effects show the impact of changes in the quality perceived by clients on business competitiveness. These effects have their source in changes in client behavior and their level of satisfaction which, ultimately, will have a positive or negative impact on volume sales and market share due to variations in clients' willingness to pay, their purchase intentions or level of expenditure within the hotel. Internal effects refer to the influence quality has on competitiveness due to changes in the firm's production processes. Such changes have an influence on productivity input and, therefore, on the firm's production costs.

There is some research that analyses both effects. The latter studies are descriptive works which do not empirically verify - through appropriate statistical analysis - the causal relationships proposed. On the other hand, the work provides a systematic compilation of the main effects of quality on different business economic indicators, such as price, market share, production costs, labor productivity, total productivity, and business returns. However, his work has an important limitation in that it does not specify the simultaneous relationships existing between the variables included; in other words, it only deals with the direct effects of quality on these economic indicators.

The endogenous and exogenous variables used in the model can be grouped into three categories. The first one includes the service quality variable, measured through a perceived quality indicator based on the level of customer satisfaction (QI). The second category refers to financial and economic variables created from the hotels' balance sheet and includes: price of the service (P), market share (MS), occupancy level (OL), average direct cost (DC), average indirect cost (IC), and returns per room, which is the proxy variable used to quantify competitiveness. The third category includes structural variables associated with the size of the hotel (S) and the number of employees per room (ER).

The occupancy level of the hotel will also have an impact on the selling price of the service. In low season periods, the hospitality sector tends to reduce the average price of their service by selling promotional packages to targeted groups or other kinds of offers. The opposite strategy is used during high demand seasons, when the hotels are able to fill all their rooms at considerably higher prices. Indeed, price policies in the hospitality sector are conditioned not only by the internal factors of the actual firm - such as costs and profit expectations - but also by demand factors. Among the latter factors, market share and seasonal variations - measured by the evolution of the occupancy level of the hotel - are highly relevant. The relationship existing between occupancy level and the price of the service is expressed by the parameter β_{OLP}, while the parameter ßMSP expresses the effect of market share on such variable.

The system of simultaneous equations resulting from the specification of the model proposed is presented in Table 1.

Table 1. Equations

$P = \alpha_p \cdot QI + \beta_{DCP} \cdot DC + \beta_{MSP} \cdot MS + \beta_{OLP} \cdot OL + u_1$	Equation [1]
$DC = \alpha_{DC} \cdot QI + \beta_{SDC} \cdot S + \beta_{ERDC} \cdot ER + \beta_{OLDC} \cdot OL + u_2$	Equation [2]
$MS = \alpha_{MS} \cdot QI + \beta_{PMS} \cdot P + \beta_{OLMS} \cdot OL + \beta_{SMS} \cdot S + u_3$	Equation [3]
$R = \alpha_R \cdot QI + \beta_{DCR} \cdot DC + \beta_{MSR} \cdot MS + \beta_{PR} \cdot P + \beta_{OLR} \cdot OL + \beta_{ICR} \cdot IC + u_4$	Equation [4]

Equation 1 is based on the model of hedonic prices suggested by Rosen and on Lancaster's consumer theory. According to this theory, consumer willingness to pay, $P_i(Z_i, Y_1)$, depends on the characteristics of the service

(Z_i), as well as on a set of consumer characteristics such as income, preferences, educational level, etc., which are encompassed by vector Y_1. Given the lack of data regarding the characteristics of the clients of the hotels under study, it was not possible to apply any kind of segmenting criteria to the demand in order to establish the *price of the service.* The optimum price set by sellers, $P_2(Z_i, Y_2)$, is not only conditioned by the characteristics of the service, Z_i, but also by some structural variables specific to each hotel, i.e., the *occupancy level* and the *market share.* Such variables, included in vector Y_2, have an effect on production costs, and consequently, on the pricing mechanism used by the hotel.

In order to analyze the influence of *service quality* on the *price of the service,* Rosen suggested constructing a quality indicator (QI) from the numerical value of the characteristics offered by such a service, $QI=f(Z_i)$. Consequently, both the price the client is willing to pay and the price the seller is willing to set will depend on the quality of the service. This direct relationship between *service quality* and the *price of the service* is expressed by the parameter α_P.

The *occupancy level* of the hotel will also have an impact on the selling price of the service. In low season periods, the hospitality sector tends to reduce the average price of their service by selling promotional packages to targeted groups or other kinds of offers. The opposite strategy is used during high demand seasons, when the hotels are able to fill all their rooms at considerably higher prices. Indeed, price policies in the hospitality sector are conditioned not only by the internal factors of the actual firm — such as costs and profit expectations — but also by demand factors. Among the latter factors, *market share* and seasonal variations — measured by the evolution of the *occupancy level* of the hotel — are highly relevant. The relationship existing between *occupancy level* and the *price of the service* is expressed by the parameter α_{OLP}, while the parameter âMSP expresses the effect of *market share* on such variable.

Among the internal factors, the most relevant is the production costs of the firm, $C(QI,Y_2)$. In this study, production costs have to be broken down into direct and indirect costs. An increment in these costs will generate an increase in the price of the service, and so the parameter β_{DCP} must take a positive value. Pricing by using a mark-up makes it possible to also cover average indirect costs. Although these costs have an effect on the returns per room via the parameter β_{ICR}, they will not have an effect on the pricing of the service.

The Spanish Association of Accounting and Business Administration (AECA) confirms this by advising the incorporation of indirect costs as product costs only in certain analyses - such as returns - but not for pricing purposes. Equation specifies the explanatory variables of average direct costs. One of the issues that has raised great interest in the literature is the analysis of the effects of service quality on business costs. The direct relationship between service quality (QI) and direct costs per room, $DC(QI,Y_2)$ is expressed by the parameter aDC. If this parameter takes a positive value, it means that it is expensive for the business to increase the level of service quality, as argued by neoclassical models.

According to this model, as workers' experience increases and the management system improves, enhancing the quality of the service becomes increasingly less expensive. This proposal is compatible with the management systems based on quality total costs. Average direct costs will not only be conditioned by service quality, but also by occupancy level and the structural variables characteristic of each hospitality firm -expressed by vector Y_2, $DC(QI,Y_2)$.

One of the most pioneering works concerning the effect of occupancy level on direct costs per room. According to these authors, an increase in the level of occupancy causes a reduction in the direct costs per room, and therefore β_{OLDC} will have a negative value. This is due to the fact that, as sales increase - in this case the level of occupancy - the negotiation conditions with providers improve and labor costs per room decline due to the increase in productivity.

Among the structural variables, the number of employees per room is especially relevant to the structure of the business' direct costs. The effect of this variable is expressed by the parameter β_{ERDC}. This parameter should be negative and is especially important in the hospitality industry, labor productivity has an increasing effect on the average direct costs as they are used in the production process. This situation is typical in luxury hotels characterized by the use of intensive labor.

Equation 3, analyzes the determinants of the hotel's market share. The direct effect of service quality on this variable is shown by parameter α_{MS}. Its sign is positive, since an increase in quality will generate an increase in sales due to client loyalty and gaining new clients. Investigated this relationship via the increase in client satisfaction and their purchase intentions. Besides service quality, other variables, such as the size of the hotel, occupancy level, and price of the service, will have an effect on market share. An increase in the size of the hotel will allow an increase in sales, as it will now have greater capacity, and so α_{SMS} must have positive values. The parameter β_{OLMS} will also have positive values, since the increase in sales associated with a greater occupancy level increases the market share of the hotel. The effect of the price of the service on the market share is less than the impact of service quality on market share.

The expected value for the parameter β_{PMS} is positive or negative depending on whether the demand is inelastic or elastic, respectively, on the assumption that the price policy of a given hotel does not have an effect on total market volume sales. Equation 4, allows us to estimate the direct effect of service quality on business competitiveness measured by the returns per room. Normally, leading firms - i.e., those with a large market share- implement more efficient management systems, their degree of vertical integration tends to be very high, and their investments, including those in R&D, are also strong.

On the other hand, the effect of occupancy levels on the returns per room in the hotel sector -whose demand is highly seasonal-is very important due to the excess of supply during low-season periods, which can decrease returns and cause important structural and financial problems. The effect of price of the service on returns per room is given by the parameter α_{PR}. The direct effect of price on business returns is due to its impact on total income. An increase in price causes an increase in total income, as long as the demand price elasticity is less than the unit in absolute terms, and so the parameter involved will have a positive value. The opposite takes place if the demand is elastic, in which case β_{PR} takes a negative value. If the increase in price is driven by an increase in average direct costs, this cost increase has a negative effect on returns per room since β_{DCR} has to be negative.

Finally, it is necessary to include in the analysis of returns the negative effect of average indirect costs on this variable. Although these costs should not be taken into account for pricing, they are essential when the analysis focuses on business returns. The theoretical model presented here will be used to test a series of hypotheses which are highly relevant to business and useful for designing new initiatives in tourism policy.

Data Source and Perceived Quality Indicator

The structural and the financial and economic variables of the model were created from the monthly data provided by 17 four- and five-star hotels -corresponding to 1997, 1998 and 1999-, and belonging to a large chain in Andalusia. The criteria described in Table 2 were used to this end. The perceived quality indicator was created from the information provided by the client surveys carried out by the hotels during the same period. The concept of perceived quality has been intensively discussed in the literature.

Some point out, this term is usually defined as "A global evaluative opinion from the clients that reflect their attitude towards the excellence or the superiority of the product in relation to their needs." From this definition, it can be deduced that perceived quality is a highly subjective judgment. In addition, this concept has a global character, despite being defined by the characteristics of the service. Finally, it is a relative indicator of quality, since it depends on the interaction between the client and the service received. The client survey carried out by each hotel served to create the indicators of perceived quality as it provides information concerning the opinions of clients about the services received, especially room, food and beverages, and reception services as well as lounges and other communal areas services.

The measurement for each of the service features was based on a scale of five: very satisfactory, satisfactory, acceptable, unsatisfactory, and very unsatisfactory. The most relevant aspects of the sample design are shown in Table 2.

Table 2. Technical file

Scope of the research	*4- and 5-star hotels in Andalusia*		
Population	*Clients of hospitality services*		
Period	1997	1998	1999
Size of the sample (1)	24,422	14,397	15,794
Sample error	10%	10%	10%
Level of confidence	95%	95%	95%

The construction of the perceived quality indicator (QI), uses the Lancaster model as the theoretical framework. From this model Rosen developed a pricing model for differentiated markets and defined quality of service indicators (QI) from the set of characteristics the service includes (Z); thus QI=f(Z). The dimensions of such indicators are created by classifying the attributes into categories with the use of exploratory or confirmatory analysis techniques. Confirmatory analysis techniques allow the researcher to define a priori the dimensions of service quality. based on theoretical knowledge or on previous empirical research.

The quality indicator is created using Structural Equation Modelling (S.E.M.). S.E.M. models are second-generation multivariate analysis techniques since they involve generalizations and extensions of first-generation techniques, and thus they allow the estimation and validation of models with both latent (i.e., unobserved) variables - such as service quality dimensions or the indicator of perceived quality -and measured (i.e., observed) variables - such as clients' opinions regarding the characteristics of the service. Using S.E.M. models, the relative weighs (a_{ij}) of the service characteristics (Z_{ij}) - included in each dimension (D_j) - can be quantified as well as the effect of each dimension on the indicator of perceived quality (β_j). In this way, the key aspects involved in client satisfaction can be elucidated in order to take the relevant steps to increase them.

The maximum likelihood method is used for the estimation, opting for the standardized solution of parameters α_{ij} and β_j. Before estimating the model, a preliminary study of the correlation matrices for those characteristics belonging to the same dimension was carried out. This information was used to eliminate from the dimension those characteristics that caused high correlations (>0.85) with other characteristics - thus preventing possible multicolinearity problems. Similarly, those characteristics were eliminated that did not yield statistically significant differences in the perceived quality indicator.

The estimation of model reveals the relative importance of each quality dimension linked to the four services provided by the hotel regarding the perceived quality indicator. The dimension that made the greatest contribution to client satisfaction was lounge and other communal areas services (0.99), followed by room services (0.87), food and beverage services (0.77), and reception/check-in services (0.76). The scores given to these coefficients should help the hotel management to reflect upon the core services they offer and therefore on which area improvement should be focussed.

Cultural Dimensions of Hospitality Service Provision

In the provision of hospitality service for international tourists, there are several kinds of culture at work. The first of these is the culture of service, that is, the values and meanings which give to service its essential quality. In a service encounter a tourist and a waiter (for example) engage in the culture of service and the waiter performs emotional labour in addition to performing technical skills. The actors in the service encounter bring to the interaction their own ethnic identities and engage in cross - cultural communication. To ensure the provision of appropriate hospitality service human resource development must take account of the cultural dimensions of hospitality.

For several years now the founding states of the Association of Southeast Asian nations (ASEAN) have made inbound international tourism an important economic activity. With their abundance of cultural and natural attractions they have lured tourists from a variety of culturally diverse generating regions. Great progress has been made since 1958 when Checci and Company, in association with the United States Depart of Commerce and pacific Area Travel Association, began an investigation of the potential for tourism in the Asia - pacific region. At that time tourism in Indonesia was virtually non - existent. At the same time the

Government of Singapore had eliminated its tourism program on the grounds that tourism was "frivolous" and "too vague" to be of use to the economy. According to the Checci Report, in 1959 the Thai government had only recently begun to see tourism as an important source of jobs, foreign exchange and income and had accordingly taken action by forming the Tourist Organization of Thailand.

The pursuit of inbound tourism as a prominent component of national economic life has, in recent years, not been confined to the foundation members of ASEAN. While those states have continued to expand their frontiers of tourism to provide new attractions for tourists, other Southeast Asian states have begun to pursue economic diversification through international tourism.

For various reasons these states, until recently, had not been prime destinations for travellers. For more than two decades Myanmar's pursuit of the isolationist Burmese Way to Socialism deprived international tourists of the chance of extended stay during which to experience the country's cultural and natural attractions. Now Myanmar seeks tourists to enhance its economic positions ant its international reputation.

Another perhaps surprising newcomer to the business of attracting tourists is the conservative oil-rich Islamic state of Brunei which according to Roger Mitton, is in the process of becoming a 'hip tourist destination' in order to diversify its economy. Mitton reports that the sultanate is 'loosening up' in order to become 'a fun place to visit.'

Vietnam and Laos are also now open for tourist business after years of Cold War conflict and economic rigidity. Their Indochinese neighbour, Cambodia, was identified by the Checchi Report as the single greatest potential tourist attraction in Southeast Asia because of the remains of the Khmer civilisation at Angkor. Unfortunately, however, continued political instability, by creating a perception of danger, so far prevents it from realising its full potential as a tourist destination. According to Kim, international tourism growth in the Asia - Pacific region is anticipated to rise to approximately 200 million visitor arrivals by the year 2000. It should come as no surprise, therefore, that the tourism and hospitality industry will be a major employer of labour.

Need for Quality Service

According to the World Travel and Tourism Council (WTTC) the Asia Pacific region's tourism industry is still in its infancy and therefore the full impact of tourism is yet to be realised. Whilst tourism growth in the region provides cause for optimism, it has already created labour supply problems for employers. By 2004, Metzger estimates that 122 million jobs will be created in Asia alone and if a consistently high level of service is to be maintained across all sectors of the industry, some 122 million skilled workers will have to be found to deliver tourism service.

Economically, much is at stake in the region if its service providers fail to meet the demands of its tourists. For example, the gross output in Thailand for 1996 from tourism was estimated to be 8.5 billion United States dollars. Due to continuing economic uncertainties in Thailand, tourism authorities are likely to seek an increase in this figure due to the need for additional foreign exchange.

Although current economic conditions in Japan are affecting outbound tourism in that country resulting in more Japanese taking their holiday at home, nevertheless Ilakim believes that, so far as outbound Japanese tourism is concerned, the majority of the jobs catering for their needs will be in the customer contact area. It is here that there will be a need for host countries in the Asia-Pacific region to have customer contact people who can communicate effectively and sensitively with the Japanese.

According to Yee the competitive edge of an economy is not found in its commodities or low wage labour, but in the contribution of a rising quality labour which can provide high levels of service. Thus the notion of quality service will play a crucial role in the economic contribution of tourism and hospitality to the region. As quality service is possibly the foremost determinant of success in the tourism and hospitality business it is important that the focus be placed on improving service. If more tourists are to be attracted to the region, it is imperative that the strategy is not put in jeopardy by the lack of quality service. It is, however, one thing to identify the need for quality service, but it is entirely another matter as to how such a service might be supplied.

The tourism and hospitality industry in the Asia Pacific region has an image problem which results in government, employers and prospective employees all sharing reservations about the nature of the industry itself. For example, the industry is perceived by potential employees as being dominated by expatriate staff in its key managerial and professional positions thereby offering limited career opportunities to the domestic work force. It is also perceived as offering low status employment for young adults or marginally skilled workers, a situation which may well lead governments to conclude that it is a minor player in the economic life of a countr. Its poor image as an employer is reinforced when students undertake work experience during their industry placements.

Certain lessons might be drawn for the region from the Hong Kong experience. Yee reports that in Hong Kong some students in tourism and hospitality are so negatively affected by their hotel placement that they choose not to enter the industry because they feel they are being used as cheap labour or as fodder for the operational needs of the hotel.

One conclusion that might be drawn from this example is that hotels do not see in the students the future of the industry itself and do not see service to the student in the same light as service to the paying customer. This lack of service to the student appears to emanate from areas of the hotel industry that should know better, namely the Human Resource (HR) people and departmental heads who apparently believe students are incapable of thinking through a problem with which they are confronted. Given such an image, the issue of the industry being able to recruit talent and expertise to its ranks is a very serious matter indeed. If talented potential employees believe there is little or no opportunity for recognition, advancement and reward, then the question must be asked as to the calibre of employees ultimately recruited to serve the ever expanding tourist market. Fortunately there are bright spots in this disturbing picture when it comes to the recruitment and placement of people in the industry.

Lessons may be learned from the approach of a Taiwanese hotel to the recruitment of talented employees. This involved the use of a variety of marketing approaches involving direct mail, flyers, window displays, magazine articles, hotel tours, school presentations, exhibition booths, and an internship program. Through these means potential employees have been attracted to a career in the hotel industry. There is also a 'Casual Club' to recruit part-time workers, giving these people a sense of belonging to the hotel. Whilst the marketing of recruitment seems reasonably well handled among employers of the region, more attention appears to be needed in the area of effective selection and placement of employees.

There is no doubt that the region has been experiencing labour shortages particularly in the areas of managerial, professional, skilled and semi-skilled labour, and to a lesser extent of unskilled labour. Whilst cross border labour movement is in part offsetting labour shortages. labour movements are increasingly likely to pose problems for some parts of the region as countries struggle to ensure that jobs are available for their own nationals who have become unemployed by the current economic crisis.

The current emphasis on management training to the detriment of skilled, semi-skilled and unskilled jobs raises the question as to just how well non-managerial employees in hospitality are being prepared to provide customer service There is also the question of how well the existing service is being delivered and whether visitors leave with a favourable impression of a destination as well as a desire to visit the destination again.

Kinds of Culture at Work

In the provision of hospitality service there are several kinds of culture at work.

The culture of service

In relation to hospitality provision the culture of service refers to the values and meanings which underlie hospitality and give it its essential quality. Essential to hospitality are the reception and entertainment of guests who are to be provided with psychological and physiological comfort and security.

Hospitality includes both tangible and intangible services. When a service encounter takes place between a tourist and a waiter (for example), both are engaging in the culture of service. In performing the required technical skill for serving the food and drink, the waiter provides the tangible service. The social interaction between the waiter and the tourist is the intangible service and contributes to the tourist's total experience. According to Powers, the social interaction requires genuine warmth and friendliness and necessitates empathy.

This section argues that service is a process which can be described using the following model.

The Service Process

Input	*Process*	*Output*	*Outcomes*
Supplier of the service	Service provision is a situational social process provided at an appropriate level and catering for individual needs.	Food, drink, accommodation and intangible benefits (such as anticipation of needs).	Quality service resulting in return visits from tourists.

This kind of labour in which emotion plays a key role is referred to as emotional labour. Hochschild sees it as exploitation of emotion. She describes it as labour that 'calls for the coordination of mind and feeling' for the purpose of producing 'the proper state of mind in others'. According to John Urry, the establishment of a contrived emotional relationship through emotional labour is 'difficult and demanding, under-recognised and relatively under-rewarded.' The relationship is also an unequal relationship between the recipient of the service who is dependent on the service job for employment.

The culture of identity

The actors in the service encounter bring to the interaction their own ethnic/national identities. Using the language of the computer age, Geert Hofstede describes this kind of culture as 'the collective programming of the mind which distinguishes the members of one group or category of people from another'. The programming involves the establishment within the person of 'patterns of thinking, feeling, and potential acting' which Hofstede calls 'the software of the mind'. Culture of this kind is learned from the various groups within which a person interacts during the course of his or her lifetime. The family, for example, plays a major role in the cultural development of an individual. According to Hofstede, much of this cultural development is acquired during early childhood 'when a person is most susceptible to learning and assimilating'.

Cultural differences are demonstrated in a variety of ways. In some societies, for example, great respect is accorded to age to a degree not evident in other societies. Ideas about personal space vary from culture to culture. In some cultures, making eye contact during verbal communication is unacceptable; in other cultures eye contact is important as a sign of openness. These various examples of cultural difference are generalisations. Besides belonging to cultural groups people are also unique personalities. Uniqueness does not, however, diminish the importance of culture. According to Singer 'uniqueness does know bounds'; these bounds are set by the cultural groups with which individuals identify.

While language differences are likely to be the most obvious component of cross- cultural service encounters, there are other aspects of Hofstede's 'software of the mind' that need to be taken into account. For example, what 'collective programming of the mind' has taken place to influence the attitude of a young man or woman towards the desirability of being a waiter in a restaurant?

Anecdotal evidence from Southeast Asian tourism and hospitality students in Australia suggests that such a job is not considered desirable for its own sake. Instead it is seen as a way to make money for immediate living expenses and, in the long term, as a springboard for a managerial position. In some cases there is reluctance to learn what are considered to be the more menial hospitality skills. If the job is not highly regarded within the cultural group, how will this affect the waiter's enthusiasm for and performance in the job? There is also the likelihood that the 'collective programming of the mind' has included animosity between cultural groups. Will this animosity affect the service encounters between members of those groups?

Yuan highlights the major issues associated with the cultural dimensions of service. The service received in a host country is often judged by the tourist's own cultural standards. For example, the Asia Pacific region is host to approximately 10 million Japanese tourists each year. According to Jang there is a great chance that visitors to the region will find customer contact people either unaware of or unable to respond to their clients' needs. Tourists in foreign lands are likely to be in search of cultural knowledge and experience. Whilst this knowledge and experience is formally provided by tour operators and guides they employ, informally hospitality service providers such as waiters and receptionists may, through conversations with guests, serve as another source of cultural knowledge.

Anecdotal evidence from tourists who have visited Bali, for example, indicates service encounters in restaurants during which young Balinese waiters, anxious to practise their English, engage with guests in the exchange of knowledge about their respective cultures. In some cases friendships are formed, correspondence is exchanged and contacts are renewed on repeat visits to Bali.

In the anthropological literature, the waiter performing this role is described as a culture broker. According to social anthropologist, Naomi Brown, 'culture brokers are found in all cross-cultural situations ... amongst taxi drivers, tourist guides, tourist police, security guards, hotel workers and market vendors. They act as mediators between tourists and the resident population'. In this capacity they play an important part in enhancing the tourists' experience of a destination.

The Culture of the Organisation

In their discussion of culture within an organisation, Paul Thompson and David McHugh make reference to 'the way that management mobilises combinations of values, language, rituals and myths' in order to unlock 'the commitment and enthusiasm of employees'. They also cite Martin and Nicholls who see the outcome of a positive organisational culture in terms of the employees' 'sense of belonging to the organisation' combined with 'a sense of enrichment in the job, and confidence in management'.

While it must be pointed out that Thompson and McHugh are somewhat critical of the concept of organisational culture and its links with commitment, arguably it may be possible to draw from their descriptions dimensions of organisational culture appropriate to large and small enterprises which provide hospitality services. If the idea is accepted that the service encounter has the potential to provide intangible as well as tangible benefits, it would seem to follow that management should have in place the appropriate 'combinations of values, language, rituals and myths' to encourage 'the commitment and enthusiasm of the employees' in enhancing the tourist's total experience.

When service is examined within the context of hospitality organisations, it can involve what Kim calls affective and continuance commitment responses from employees. Kim has found that those who have positive feelings of identification and involvement with their organisation develop an emotional attachment to it. This results in employees wanting to maintain their tenure, relate positively to their customers and provide the customer with quality service. This view of service is similar to that of Urry who in part described service as involving intimacy with the customer as well as a concern in providing a quality service for the consumer.

Kim contrasts this view with what he terms continuance commitment where employees, through longevity of service and past promotions, feel trapped in their employment. If these employees left their organisation it would be at great financial and personal cost to themselves and their plateaued careers.

Continuance commitment people were found to relate less positively, and in some cases, even negatively to their customers as well as doing no more than was necessary to maintain their membership of the organisation. The implication of this study for service is that those organisations that succeed in winning emotional commitment from their employees and engage in career development are likely to be better service providers than those that have employees who feel trapped with nowhere to go. For people serving time in their organisation their own needs may become more important than serving the customer.

HRD and Hospitality Service Provision

Human Resource Development has improved performance as its ultimate goal in order to enhance the competitiveness and efficiency of an organisation. The term HRD is made up of three core components:

- training to improve the performance of employees in their current job,
- education to develop the whole person for future roles and responsibilities which as yet remain unknown, and
- development which prepares people for their responsibilities in the short to medium term of their career.

As tourism and hospitality is one of the largest and fastest growing industries in the world, it has, in the view of the WTTC, a need to address increased and improved tourism education in the region. This step is necessary in order to accommodate and adapt to ever increasing pressure on tourism and hospitality resources in the region. According to Yee HRD is one of the most widely used terms in Asia-Pacific gatherings because it is seen as central to the competitive edge of the economy of a nation.

The key HRD stakeholders in any country are its HRD providers, supporters and users in terms of government, employers, and educational institutions. Tourists also are indirectly stakeholders in that they receive the benefit or otherwise of the outcomes and effectiveness of HRD initiatives. Governments will not become involved in HRD initiatives unless they believe tourism can make a positive contribution to their economy. As tourism employs 1 in 9 of the work force of the world, and it is predicted by 2005 to contribute some 2.0 trillion dollars from travel and gross output in the Asia Pacific region. it would seem good economic sense for government to support well constructed arguments for quality improvements in the industry.

Ideally the development of a program for skills development should be a joint project for industry and vocational education which together bring to the task an understanding of the requirements of industry and an appreciation of the pedagogical factors involved in providing training for skills development. The refinement of competency- based modules and train the trainer programs in recent years means that standardised training can take place in vocational education institutions and in the workplace through on - the -job training.

Within the domain of skills development, there i5 the opportunity to empower employees by engaging them in a process of commitment to quality service When skills are applied within a Quality framework, these can be used to achieve satisfying service outcomes. If employees are engaged actively in continually improving their service processes to meet the needs of their customers, hospitality service provision will be the beneficiary.

For example, through their direct contact with customers in a bar, hospitality staff may become aware that long queues form no matter how expertly they perform their skills. Because of their first-hand knowledge of the situation, bar staff, if consulted, may recommend a change to the work process such as a series of minibars within the establishment to reduce time pressures on staff and satisfy their customers. In this instance both the customer and staff experience satisfying outcomes.

Developing a Culture of Service

Competency-based modules for skills development cannot guarantee the inculcation of the values which underpin the culture of service. Customer relations modules, through role play methodology, may attempt to develop behaviours which are supposed to indicate a commitment to the emotional content of service but such behaviours are mere surface acting and may lack the ring of sincerity.

While there are good reasons for the 'stereotyped forms of address' and the programmed presentation of service in fast food restaurants, it is unlikely that many customers take the performance seriously. Crang likens the performance of emotional labour to a theatrical event directed by management. While surface acting training is one means of preparing people for their roles as service-givers, Crang also draws attention to staff training 'in a deeper Stanislavskian level of performance', that is, deep acting which, if Hochschild's view is accepted, can have a psychologically damaging effect upon the performers because they lose touch with their true feelings. If acting, either surface or deep, is inappropriate, how then can a truly genuine culture of service be developed?

At the level of management in a hospitality enterprise there must be a genuine appreciation of the values underlying the culture of service and an understanding of what constitutes a positive total experience for guests. This genuine appreciation is reflected in the manner in which staff are recruited with attention being given to the recruitment of people with personality characteristics suitable for empathetic service provision. It is also reflected in the culture of the organisation which creates 'a sense of enrichment in the job'. These criteria for appropriate management have implications for the education of managers who, besides needing studies in business and management, would have a greater understanding of the importance of the psychosocial dimensions of hospitality provision through in-depth study of relevant social sciences such as sociology and psychology. This understanding would encompass both the psychosocial dimensions of the tourist experience as well as the need for protection of the psychological well-being of the service workers from the deleterious effects of emotional labour.

Appreciation of Cultural Diversity

The hospitality worker is likely to work in a multicultural environment. Besides the cross-cultural encounters front of house, there are also back of house encounters which have their own cultural dimension. While globalisation may result in superficial cultural homogenisation, the strength of traditional values and attitudes developed over many centuries should not be underestimated. The Chinese chef, for example, is the end result of a long established Confucian tradition which is not shared by the Irish waiter. Each is the product of a particular cultural programming.

How should hospitality workers be prepared for interactions with a multicultural clientele and a multicultural workforce? Within current hospitality education and training programs one may find components relating to cross-cultural communication. The danger with short courses such as these is that they will highlight the apparently exotic aspects of a culture and thus encourage stereotyping and ridicule.

Cross-cultural understanding may be best achieved by a long-term systematic development of cultural knowledge beginning in elementary school. Yee (1992:19) argues that any human resource development strategy in terms of the cultural dimensions of service ought to have its roots in the elementary education of a nation. Such an education should highlight humanity's shared experiences as well as cultural diversity and should span all the years of one's education.

Raising the Status of Hospitality As an Occupation

Generally service work in hospitality has low status as an occupation. At the same time the customer contact aspect of hospitality, it has been argued, plays an important role in the total tourist experience. It therefore seems imperative to take steps to raise the status of the occupation.

One way in which an attempt can be made to achieve this goal is through educational provision for careers in hospitality. While considerable attention has been given to management training, more attention needs to be given to the integration of operational training into educational programs at degree level. There are, no doubt, several ways in which this can be achieved. For example, a degree may be constructed by building a one or two-year program at university on to a two-year program at vocational college. Alternatively, a three or four-year degree program may be taken concurrently with a hospitality program at a vocational college. The latter approach has the advantage of introducing students to the culture of academic reflection from the beginning of tertiary study.

In university circles it is likely that combining vocational and academic study within a degree program will meet with some disapproval. The old status division between working with the hands and working with the mind has not disappeared. The combination of the two strands within a degree program, however, has many advantages. It supports an integrated career path for hospitality workers thus helping to overcome the perception that hospitality work is a dead-end job. It enables students who, through a relatively poor academic performance at school, did not gain entrance to university to prove their capabilities at vocational college and then to have a second chance at a university education. Lifelong learning cannot be constrained by artificial structures in education. In the vocational college component of the degree, assuming that hospitality practitioners are employed as teachers, it puts students in touch with the 'real world' of hospitality.

Self Service in Hospitality

This section makes the case for widespread deployment of self-service technologies and processes in the hospitality industry. Spurred by the success of airline check-in kiosks and seeking additional ways to cut costs and increase guest satisfaction, hoteliers will drive these solutions into properties aggressively.

Consider the case of Alex, a business traveler. Alex enters the Global Inn Chicago. His Bluetooth-enabled PDA informs him that check-in is in process and directs him to enter his Global Inn passcode. When he does his PDA indicates that he has been assigned room 835 (king, non-smoking). Alex hits "confirm," bypassing the offer to upgrade to a suite for an additional $40. One of the hotel's guest experience managers, conspicuously near the hotel entrance, greets him with a smile, asks him if he needs help with his bags and then directs him to the elevator. He notices the crowd at the new sushi bar as he walks to the elevator. He finds it amusing that the thing he likes most about this hotel replaced the thing he once liked the least—long lines at check-in. Hotel management clearly has found a better use for the space once occupied by the front desk.

Proceeding to his room, Alex notices that the PDA displays a map of the eighth floor with directions to room 835. When he gets to the door, he pulls out his credit card and swipes it through the door lock. He opens the door, drops his bags and heads right back down to the sushi bar.

Actually, this scenario is possible today—and arguably commonplace five years from now. It illustrates the power of the self-service channel as hoteliers begin to look beyond reservations and sales via the Internet—the first significant self-service opportunity in the hospitality industry—to fulfillment and guest services on property.

Consider the history and impact of self service across a number of industries. ATMs were probably the earliest avatars, appearing in 1969. Self service at the gas pump wasn't far behind, spurred by the energy crisis in the early 1970s. Self service became mainstream when consumers flocked to the Internet because of the convenience and price transparency that this channel offered. The subsequent impact to the travel industry can not be overstated. Today, kiosks are prevalent in photo shops, movie theaters, malls, the DMV and countless other consumer locations. What is the common thread? Easy access, speed, customer empowerment and cost savings for the businesses that employ them.

Are Hotels Destined to Follow Suit? We believe that hotels must. Consider the airline industry: plagued by bankruptcies in the last two years, the industry was forced to reduce costs substantially. At the same time security procedures implemented after Sept. 11 increased waiting times, so staffing reductions alone were not a feasible alternative. Airlines turned to check-in kiosks—largely because they had little choice. The results were dramatic: 30 percent cost reductions related to check-in were not uncommon. And, to the surprise of some observers, many passengers embraced this new way of checking in. But those who travel regularly were not surprised. Skeptics may argue that hotels have done kiosk trials over the years and have met with limited success; that hotels are different; that guests want and expect face-to-face service. It is true that trials over the past five years have not been entirely successful. This was due in part to immature technology, unreliable hardware, limited application functionality, ineffective marketing and low commitment from corporate management and onsite staff.

The case against self service on the grounds that guests want face-to-face service is dubious. If the experience of the airlines is not reason enough to debunk that notion, consider a 2002 study by Vanderbilt University in which 53 percent of guests indicated that they were likely to use a check-in kiosk. The study also showed that ease of check-in and check-out ranked ahead of friendly service and price on guests' wish lists.

Potential Impact of Self Service on Hospitality

Let's examine the potential impact of self service on the hospitality industry. First, an effective solution could yield significant savings through reduced front desk staffing levels. While the savings potential is greatest for large full-service or convention hotels, limited service could benefit as well, depending on the degree to which operators are willing to make the channel the primary mode of checking in. It is constructive here to note that although the airlines were at first reluctant, they have since achieved considerable savings.

Second, and perhaps more important, these solutions could increase guest satisfaction, especially for those who are inclined to self-empowerment. While the convenience of self service—eliminating or reducing lines at check-in and check-out, especially during peak periods—will appeal to many, the real power lies in what these solutions do for employees. No longer tethered to the front desk staring at a computer screen, front-line service staff can refocus on value-added guest interactions. In addition, engineered correctly, the technology can more consistently recognize guests and offer them personalized service commensurate with their value to the hotel.

Automated concierge applications will allow guests to find the information they seek easily and quickly. We anticipate that this feature will have wide-scale applicability in limited-service hotels.

Third, hotels can expect revenue uplift beyond that offered by the increased wallet share of repeat guests. The opportunity exists to consistently up-sell room categories based on yield parameters. Many airlines offer first class upgrades (typically $50 for short/medium-haul domestic trips) at check-in based on availability and have seen incremental revenue. Additionally, kiosks are also an excellent channel to make dynamic one-to-one marketing offers, such as spa, restaurant and local attraction tie-ins.

Lastly, as the scenario above illustrates, the implementation of self-service technologies and processes offers innovative hotels a fresh opportunity to rethink the use of the lobby and public spaces. Most guests really don't like the front desk. It is not difficult to envision alternative uses, such as the sushi bar noted in the opening example.

Self-Service Model

Note that the opening scenario did not mention kiosks. While kiosks will undoubtedly play a primary role on property in the near term, they will move to the background as digital wireless technologies—including WiFi and Bluetooth—gain a broader foothold and security issues are addressed. Other self-service channels will include in-room interactive television and the Web. Increasingly, these channels will blur and their differences will become irrelevant.

Therefore, it is important to adhere to an architectural model that promotes multiple channels, makes available a wide variety of applications and enables a consistent travel experience across all channels. More and more, self-service functions will not perform a single transaction, but will act on a series of interrelated decisions enacted by the customer. They will integrate business processes, customer choices, customer preferences and history, and host systems to perform end-to-end functions. In doing so, hoteliers will find that the self-service channel is not only the least expensive channel but also the one with which many guests will prefer to interact.

Hospitality Education

The relevance of hospitality education is an important issue for the industry as technology, finance and marketing become big drivers for success. The report of a recent international survey on hospitality education proves this fact. Vast majority of the survey respondents (95 percent) identified customer service as a vital educational issue - clearly a wellplaced priority that positions the customer at the center of the universe. An impressive majority of respondents (87 percent) also identified marketing as an important educational focus -

a reflection of the growing competitiveness of the industry and of its increasing orientation to the customer.

Encouraging more young people into hospitality education is clearly a top priority since a majority of respondents - 74 percent globally - agree that the industry faces a continuing shortage of qualified labor, with respondents from Asia / Pacific noting a more acute shortage than their counterparts in EMEIA. Contributing to the shortages are a variety of factors including competition from better paying industries and the hospitality industry's low compensation levels.

Training and development

As hospitality organizations plan for the training and development of their employees in the future, they will evidently need to work more on their planning process - the current view is fairly negative. While just over two-thirds of respondents agreed that their training plan was 'effective', only 18 percent could "strongly agree" with such a statement. And one-third of respondents either took no position or viewed their plan as ineffective responses which suggest plenty of room for improvement.

As to training methods - "on the job" appears to be the dominant theme, although this approach should diminish somewhat in the future. Three out of four report using mentoring and coaching today with plans to increase this in the future. Just over 70 percent report formal classroom training, and two-thirds report video-based methods with plans to significantly increase this latter form in the future. Thankfully, there is also clear evidence of a significant increase in investment in training in the future - 89 percent of our respondents report plans to increase their training budgets, with well over one -quarter of these reporting that such increases will be significant.

The direction of such expanded investments in training, however, remains of concern. Just over three quarters of our respondents report the development and use of their own training programs, suggesting that our industry probably wastes a great amount of effort in duplication. By contrast, only 18 percent report the use of "pre - packaged" industry wide training programs. We conclude here that the industry's leadership and its educators should devote more attention to this area in the future - providing more in the way of generic training solutions with industry-wide application.

Some of the more popular development programs include multi-skilling, cross-training and career succession - and there are clear plans to significantly expand their use in the future. There also appears to be widespread use of employee participation programs - close to two-thirds of respondents cite the use of suggestion schemes - a fairly traditional approach, while a surprisingly high 46 percent indicate job enrichment programs and 43 percent so-called "quality circles". Some 29-32 percent of respondents indicate use of autonomous work groups, work councils and self directed work teams. Looking into the future, there should be large increases in all such employee participation programs.

Hospitality organizations also use a variety of methods to identify workplace issues and for the most part intend to significantly increase their use in the future. Employee surveys, currently used by 70 percent of respondents, are planned for an increase in the future (by 79 percent). And while 68 percent of respondents acknowledge the use of suggestion boxes - the "employee" equivalent of the guest comment card - use of these passive instruments is expected to decline in the future.

Improving Performance

As human capital becomes more expensive to recruit, train and develop, increasing attention is being devoted to those factors that affect productivity. Empowerment, education, training, recognition programs and technology will all play different roles in this area in the future. The area with greatest prospective impact on productivity appears not surprisingly, to be training (cited by 94 percent). Three out of four respondents held that empowerment, education, career advancement, incentive and recognition programs would also have strong impacts on productivity in the future. Somewhat less impactful (although still indicated by a relatively high 70 percent of respondents), was the role of technology.

Following the identification of those factors that will contribute to productivity improvement in the future, we were interested in determining how productivity had changed, if at all, over the last three years. The results were surprising. No fewer than 22 percent of our respondents reported a decline in productivity. The Americas were the big standout with 29 percent of respondents reporting reduced productivity, while 14 percent and 13 percent respectively of respondents from EMEIA and Asia / Pacific cited declines. These responses indicate that in the Americas at least, some of the big productivity gains that were made in the early 1990's under pressures of falling occupancies and disappearing profits, have now been given up as revenues have soared upwards and profits have returned.

Employee Satisfaction and Performance

In view of the evident relationship between employee and customer satisfaction, our respondents were asked to rank the different approaches to improving the former. Predictably, the list was led by compensation, although our respondents anticipate this will become less important in the future. Employee recognition programs, the opportunity for career advancement and exposure to training followed in order of impact.

Improving performance is desirable but it also needs to be measured. And while most organizations tend to rely heavily on an employee's immediate supervisor for performance review, the increasing popularity of alternative systems such as self, peer and subordinate review to provide "360 degree feedback" are well worth noting as are those involving customers.

Although many would acknowledge the validity of the relationship between customer and employee satisfaction and in turn their relationship to financial performance, only 45 percent of our respondents report an integrated measurement system to account for these factors. In developing an integrated measurement system, the first step is to develop an accurate accounting of employee satisfaction. And to this end, a variety of methods are reportedly used.

The leading yardstick appears to be employee turnover - now used by 81 percent of respondents, although this should decline in the future as a greater reliance is placed on other methods. Employee surveys are destined for much greater usage in the future (by more than 55 percent). And finally, upward evaluations now used by 18 percent are expected to more than double in use in the future.

Good Performance Deserves Reward

Dominating the incentive programs in the hospitality industry are cash bonuses, reported by 83 percent of respondents, although there are clear plans to moderate their use in the future. While a minority report use of stock options (18 percent) and team-based pay (19 percent), utilization of these methods is expected to rise dramatically in the future - to 37 percent and 41 percent respectively. For those employees who perform well, there are also various "non-monetary" recognition programs in place throughout the industry as evidenced by the 61 percent of respondents who indicated that their organizations had comprehensive "non monetary" recognition plans in place.

Table 3. Incentive programs

	Today	Future
Cash Bonuses	83%	78%
Profit / gain sharing	31%	58%
Team Based Pay	19%	41%
Spot Cash Awards	39%	40%
Stock Options	18%	37%
Don't Know / No Answer	2%	4%
No Incentive Programs	7%	1%

"Hospitality 2000 - The People" has identified what we believe will be the defining issues in the management of the hospitality industry's human capital resources in the next millennium. Hospitality organizations around the globe appear to have set their priorities and will hopefully pursue these with the same vigor that they have historically applied in other areas of this complex capital and people intensive business. And for those that do, they will be in a far better position to compete in a world market space where human relationships and information will be valued far more highly than the physical assets that have been so central a part of the industry's makeup and psyche in the past.

Competencies for a Hospitality Management Career

The importance of hospitality and tourism management education has been recognized globally. Many years now, hospitality and tourism education plus formal education provide significantly, skilled human resources. In popular tourism destination countries like Greece for example, hospitality and tourism education systems have been developed, in order to come up to the expectations of tourism and hospitality industry. The responsibility of developing tourism and hospitality management human resources lies within the hospitality organizations and within the education system of the country.

In order to achieve the objective of the provision of skilled and competent human resources, the role of formal education is significant. The responsibility and value of hospitality management education in Greece, is of crucial importance in the means of provision of proper human resources. This is enforced with the fact that the satisfaction of tourists' needs depends largely on the human resources available skills.

According to Mariger and Miller, in the environment of contemporary global business, the majority of tourism business requires human resources to be educated. Moreover, some argue that due to the complexity of the tourism industry in relation to continuous tourism management needs, it is imperative that industry executives develop their knowledge skills. The development of value-adding skills of human resources contributes to the success of the tourism or hospitality business.

To facilitate a clear view of the nature of tourism and hospitality management education and training, it is important to distinguish the differences between the education and training. Some states that, universities provide education and educational system of a country while training is generally provided by the industry. Furthermore, education has been defined as a field of multidisciplinary study, which brings the perspectives of many disciplines, especially those found in the social sciences, to bear on particular areas of application and practice in hospitality and tourism industry. John Dewey, the American philosopher, has defined education as follows:

> "It is that recognition or reorganization of experience which adds to the meaning of experience, and which increases ability to direct the course of subsequent experience".

Some argued that "training and development refers to a planned effort by an organization to facilitate the learning of job-related behaviour on the part of its employees". The concept of training includes all formal learning actions, which may perhaps, or not lead to qualifications and possibly will be obtained at any time in a working line of business.

Competencies based Curriculum Debate

According to the diverse nature of the hospitality industry, it is not easy to precisely define what skills and competencies a hospitality management graduate may need. Tas asserts that graduates should have a multi-skills base, which allows them to be creative, flexible and adaptable. The issue of how to design optional programs stayed unsolved in the 1970s and 1980s. Since the 1970s, some trade experts have criticized hotel and restaurant education as being out of touch with the needs of industry.

A number of four-year hospitality programs began to respond to the demand for increased professional skills by focusing on the particular needs of the hospitality industry. In addition to the above issue, the need for redesigning the hospitality curriculum has been established by many researchers as well. While, Lewis examined the need to readdress curricula by expressing the concern that present programs will not continue to exist if they will not be re-evaluated by taking into consideration the changing managerial and social needs.

In providing a useful typology, Cooper and Lockwood put in plain words three ways in which the study of tourism has developed as an academic subject. Primarily, it was through specific training related to the travel sector, by courses in the business area, and subsequently by the study of tourism, which was approached in conjunction with traditional subjects such as geography, sociology and linguistics. The development of tourism education is challenging due to the segmented nature of the subject, being both inter and multi-disciplinary adding to conflict and miscomprehension.

Tas investigated the management competencies essential for graduate trainees in the hotel industry according to the views of the general managers of top American hotels. Tas defines competencies as activities and skills, which are essential in order to perform the duties of a specific position. Tas' is considered as groundbreaking and pioneering examinations of hospitality management competencies.

Tas's study in Britain and Christou and Eaton carried out the same research in Greece in 1996 examining the European dimension regarding the industry expectations of education for hotel management competencies. Essential competencies in the hospitality industry are practically different from those in the educational institutions. What competencies employees consider to be optional has been asked along with a number of management groups and the answer has changed over time. In the late 1970s and early 1980s, investigators' outcomes appeared to centre more on technical matters than the answers found in the studies of the late 1980s and after.

Tas, believes the important competencies in hospitality industry are:

— Managing the guest problems with understanding and sensitivity;

— Maintaining professional and ethical standards in the work environment;

— Demonstrating poise and a professional appearance;

— Communicating electively both in writing and orally;

— Developing positive customer relations; and

— Striving to achieve the positive working relationships with employees.

Tas, furthermore, stresses that important competencies for hotel-manager trainees are:

— Human relations skills;

— Professional ethical standards;

— Diplomacy;

— Elective oral and written communication skills.

Moreover, researchers until 1990 include technical, human, and conceptual and demonstration of organization skills, people skills, and leadership as important competencies. Moreover, on the hotel managers' expectations on graduate entrants to the industry in the U.K identified the following most important competencies:

— Management of guest problems with understanding and sensitivity;

— Effective communication in both written and oral form;

— Achievement of positive working relationships with employees;

— Professional appearance and poise;

— Development of positive customer relations;

— Motivations of employees to achieve desired performance;

Particularly Sandwith expanded the Katz's three dimensions model and expounded the competency-domain model with the five elements to include:

— Conceptual-creative, which known as the cognitive;

— Leadership, that is the ability to turn ideas into productive action;

— Interpersonal, referred to those skills for elective interaction with others;

— Administrative, regarding personnel and financial management of the business; and

— Technical, concerning the knowledge and skills essential to producing the product or service.

Lewis put a greater emphasis on conceptual skills too. Although quite a lot of authors tend to believe leadership as a human skill, it is considered that a basic skill in leadership, which leadership is a person's ability to generate a vision for the future. Human relation skill is an additional vital interior competency, which is supported by many authors. Interpersonal competency and teamwork ranked most highly along with elective communication when recruiters make selection decisions. Supervisory personnel claimed that they needed additional professional development training in many human resource skills.

The importance of food and beverage competencies expected of hospitality management graduates as perceived by hospitality practitioners, educators, and students, indicated that human-relations and managerial skills were once again counted essential for students graduating from hospitalitymanagement programs.

Some argue that hospitality students require a real and in-depth understanding of the industry and HRM issues within it from a theoretical and conceptual point of view before they are given operational and prescriptive models of how to operate within that environment. Moreover, Baum and Nickson suggest for a stronger pedagogical basis to the learning experience with which students are confronted in the human resource management area of the hospitality-tourism curriculum.

According to the same survey, the programme should focus on seven key themes:

— Strategic orientation or the capability to see the big picture;

— Communications ability;

— Management style, principally working as teams;

— Leadership skills such as the ability to persuade, motivate and encourage;

— Analytical ability and sufficient mastery of technical skills and industry concepts to couple knowledge with excellence in implementation;

— Ethical awareness; and

— International scope.

Mainly in terms of management evaluation of accomplishment, autonomy, discipline and high work ethics. Furthermore, Umbreit has described the six most interesting content areas for hospitality curricula that are the human resources management, service marketing, leadership, financial analysis, interpersonal skills and Total Quality Management. Results of the survey suggest that the hospitality educators in the future may have to consider ways of enriching the students' potential to manage guest problems with understanding and sensitivity.

Thus, some suggest, hospitality management students need to receive basic knowledge in business principles, a liberal-arts education for general development and a semi-technical knowledge in addition to an application of business principles through the hospitality establishments. It could also be examined if it is necessary to introduce more sophisticated forms of teaching like 'laboratory sessions' allowing students to study the connection linking theoretical concepts and the real world.

Essential Competencies required by the Industry

The significance of the difficulties in defining what skills and competencies a hospitality management graduate may need because of the diverse nature of the hospitality industry was discussed during the literature review was the. In addition, the need for redesigning the hospitality curriculum has been established by many researchers as well. As a result, several researchers have investigated the management competencies for graduate trainees in the hotel industry, which are essential in order to perform the duties of a specific position.

Indispensable competencies in the hospitality industry differ from those in the educational institutions. The competencies that employees consider to be optional have been questioned along with a number of management groups and the answer has changed over time. However, plenty of essential skills and competencies have been recommended from many researchers, depending on the sample and the location that their research took place.

As mentioned by Christou, educators seemed to be inadequate in terms of teaching experience and skills, failing thus to meet the present and the future educational needs. The learning materials were also poor in terms of providing educational knowledge. Although education seems to be efficient in providing the industry with employees, it does not look capable enough to supply the hospitality labour market with skilled and qualified human resources.

In order to improve these theoretical topics, respondents have suggested that both educational materials and educators need improvements and further development. Like industry professionals, hospitality educators must also stay one step ahead of the competition if education is to keep up with the contemporary economic environment. General recommendations made by the respondents for their courses and studies such as the creation of school-based projects that required them to work in teams or to do research for industrial contacts.

Concerning the level of the essential skills required by the industry that the establishments offer, they need further development and improvements in reference to respondents' perceptions. The vast majority of the respondents' were not satisfied by their improvements in those skills. According to the respondents' perceptions, in order that educators improve the soft skills, emphasis should be given on creating forms of learning role-plays, case studies, simulations, out of class assignments, business games internships and psychodrama. Similar learning methods have been used in a variety number of hospitality and tourism management courses throughout the word.

3

Information Technology in Hospitality Marketing

The process of accelerating globalisation resulted in numerous considerations, one of these being: "Globalisation has also changed international tourism. The market has experienced an enormous increase and new destinations are constantly appearing on the market. Large tourist enterprises have been established which are doing business independent from states and have their branch-offices in all parts of the world. Thanks to new technologies, these enterprises can offer standard and homogenous product. In this way, tourism is greatly influenced by globalisation."

The travel industry is affected by increased competition through globalisation, diversified customer dcrnands and expectations, as well as growing of computer-based knowledge. On the other hand, it is obvious that exactly the changes caused by globalisation at first and at most affect the inunediate holders of business activities within the travel sector. While thriving to be competitive in the global market, exactly the hospitality industry is exposed and overburdened by exclusively high costs for:

— promotion in the global market,
— inunediatc communication / interactivity with the clients / tourists,
— booking by guests from distant tourist generating destinations,
— market research.

The costs mentioned above can be reduced by usllig WWW in tourism business. Namely, the Internet and its application (WWW) have created information infrastrrrettrrc which now rivals the Plain Old Telephone System (POTS) and other traditional ways ol perfornung business in size, coverage and popularity. However, some authors emphasize the uncertainty of reacting of potential guests from all over the world to the change of information and distribution medium, which is to help them reach desired destination. Individual experts suggested the policy and strategy, which should be adopted by developing countries in order to increase their participation in e-business in tourism, and the possible role of UNCTAD and other international organizations in developing suggested policies and strategies.

Since tourism is the leading world industry at the begiruling of the new millerrniunr, if supported by the Internet it represents the most popular e-business category, i.e. the number one on-line segment. Explosive growth of the online travel market is being expected, and it was estimated to reach $30 billion in 2000. In the enviroment of market-based economy and free trade, tourism in transitional counlires cannot `survive' without entrepreneurship programs doing business over the Internet, because today this is the only way to become an active participant in the global market. The emerging globalisation and concentration of supply increase the level of competition and require new Internet marketing strategies for destinations.

Features of Internet Enhanicng the Marketing Process

The Internet is the global 'network of networks" of interlinked computers operating on a standard protocol which allows data to be transferred between them. As an information exchange system, the most important aspect of the Internet is its connectivity, the ability to allow everyone to access the network. The potential of using the Internet for marketing activities is derived from its general use as an information exchange system in the digital age. The information can be stored, indexed, retrieved, restructured and redistributed automatically by software and without human intervention. The Internet connects companies with companies, companies with customers, and people with people without regard to time, space and hardware/ software platforms.

Although the Internet originated in the 19605, it is only in recent years that it has become a buzz-word. Internet services fall into two broad categories: communication services and information services. Communication services such as e-mail, and e-mail-based discussion lists and net news, allow the direct exchange of information between Internet users. Information services, including Telnet, Gopher and anonymous FTP (the File Transfer Protocol), allow users to access data that has been made available by other users. Since 1993, the Internet has been transformed completely by its newest component the World Wide Web (WWW or the

Web). The WWW not only integrates other file transfer protocols like Gopher and FTP, but also allows the user to access hosts through Telnet, read newsgroups and use e-mail. Through an Internet browser, a user can link to any web sites and may explore the Internet resource in an unprecedented way for both leisure and commercial purposes. Moreover, the Web's capability to blend text, pictures, sounds and video clips into multimedia documents played the key role in popularising the Internet beyond its traditionally academic boundaries and become an effective communication means in business and everyday life. Indeed, the WWW has been so successful that it changed the appearance of the Internet and for many it even become synonymous with the Internet itself.

The rapid growth of the Internet, especially the WWW, has attracted a great deal of interest among both academic researchers and business practitioners, especially in the fields of Information Technology (IT) and marketing. There are also an increasing number of publications on Internet tourism marketing, in the last few years. The works of Bender, Sheldon, Inkpen, Richer and O'Neil-Dunne, Buhalis and Schertler, Marcussen and O'Connor, among others, have provided the necessary background and some in-depth discussions of the various issues of marketing tourism on the Internet, in particular its impacts on tourism distribution. However, this field of research is, by and large, still in its infancy and much more effort must be made to improve our understanding of the Internet's role in tourism marketing and the ways through which tourism organisations and destinations can exploit its full potential.

The Internet is widely recognised as an extremely valuable marketing tool. It is generally held that the

Internet offers substantial advantages over traditional means of communication: reduced costs of information exchange; increased speed of information transfer and retrieval; increased customer involvement in and control of transactions; and greater flexibility of using the marketing mix. Its main business uses include communications, market research, customer services, market penetration, product development, cost savings through process reengineering, direct marketing, advertising and product delivering. The following paragraphs examine the main features of the Net, in comparison with conventional media and with relevance to marketing, as an effective and efficient communications means.

Addressability

The Internet has the unique quality that, through its addressibility, can transform the prominent marketing communication paradigm from one-to-many to one-to-one or from broadcasting to narrowcasting. The traditional media, such as print, radio and television, follow a passive one-to-many communication model, whereby a company reaches many current and potential customers through the broadcasting of the same message. This approach to communication has three problems:

— uncustomised message to every consumer,

— wasted exposures to uninterested audiences, and

— "noise" distraction from competing and conflicting messages.

In contrast, the Internet enables a company to individually "address" consumers in its marketing communications because each time a user visits its web site, its server has a record of the user's electronic address. The company can then "narrowcast" - send tailor-made message content - to a smaller target audience or an individual consumer.

Blattberg and Deighton argue that this kind of addressable marketing is not new; the mail, telephone and personal selling have also been the addressable tools in marketing for many years. What makes the Internet so special in this regard is its low-cost and high-speed information transmission and retrieval. The addressability of the Web provides the opportunity for marketing to create individual relationships, managing markets of one, and addressing each in terms of its stage of development.

In essence, it represents the opportunity to customise and tailor the product and/or the marketing effort to one consumer at a time. Pitta argues that this Internet-enabled one-to-one marketing reconfigures the familiar four Ps into one element - the relationship. It represents the ultimate expression of target marketing - a market of one - or at least one at a time. Therefore, well designed Internet communications, through web sites, emails and news-groups, can match the effectiveness of personal selling. In fact, Internet marketers can do what a sales-force can but with much more flexibility, better memory and less cost.

Interactivity

Another feature of the Net that distinguishes itself from traditional communication media is its ability to respond to user inputs, i.e. interactivity. The Internet is capable of giving feedback in response to the actions users perform on the computer, resulting in the sense of engagement with the computer. This two-way dialogue forms an important component of relationship marketing, and is an important factor in building customer loyalty. Customers are effortlessly communicate with companies to find product information and conduct transactions with a few keystrokes while companies can easily contact customers to clarify their needs or inform them of new products. Features such as Email, web forms and Java applets positively encourage marketers to interact with consumers.

Moreover, in contrast to traditional communication channels like newspapers or television, on the Net the customer is an active participant and is in greater control of choosing and processing information about the firm. It is the customer who decides with whom to interact and how to interact. In other words, it is entirely in the customer's power to decide whether to surf the net, which web site to visit, which web page to browse, for how long, how often and how much information to obtain.

In addition to the company-to-consumer and consumer-to-company interaction, Kiani examines the consumer-to-consumer and company-to-company communications and argues that in an interactive media like the Net, a marketing activity can employ a combination of the above communication patterns. The company-to-company interaction not only provides competitive intelligence but also provides opportunities in partnering and co-operation, especially in improving supply-channel and distribution-channel relationships. The consumer-to-consumer communication helps to establish cyber or virtual communities, which has significant implications for marketing segmentation and customer service. These online "clubs" can be an important venue for consumers to exchange information or experiences, for example opportunities in time-sharing accommodation, as well as for companies to improve the understanding of consumer behaviour.

Flexibility

The Web is a much more flexible marketing medium than the traditional mass media. A web page can be considered as an electronic billboard, electronic advertisement, or electronic catalogue that provides information on products or services plus contact information for interested consumers. But a virtual advertisement or catalogue is much flexible than a physical advertisement or catalogue. It can gather fresh and updated information based on the direct feedback received from consumers. A virtual catalogue can be gradually developed and organised based on the actual interest of consumers. It can also keep consumers constantly informed of the company's new product offerings, latest price changes and sales promotion initiatives.

In the travel business, the Web's flexibility and instantaneousness in information transmission is invaluable, since where the brochure is the main means for marketing package tours. UK tour operators, for example, produce about 120 million holiday brochures a year, 40% of which are not used at all. For some holidays it takes, in average, 28 brochures to generate a booking. In addition, large tour operators usually launch their main summer holiday brochures 10 months in advance . Obviously, the preparation and distribution of holiday brochures is a costly and lengthy process during which the demand conditions and competition situation could change greatly. With the print medium, tour operators have to issue supplements to the main brochures, adjusting prices and availability. With the Web, all changes to the electronic brochures can be made instantly and at little cost. The online brochure can also be linked to inventory data, so that the user can immediately see whether a particular holiday is available or not. Moreover, the electronic brochure can be indexed in many ways and the user can be provided with search facilities to locate items quickly. They can also be associated with relevant free information and services for the consumer who visits the page.

Accessibility

As a communication medium, the area in which the Internet has overwhelming advantage over any other media is its permanent exposure and global market reach. The Net greatly improves, both spatially and temporally, the information availability and user interaction. With an effective web site, a company is on business on a global spectrum 24 hours a day, 365 days a year. Any web user in the world can access its marketing information at any time that is convenient for him. This extends greatly the place and time utility of companies which traditionally rely on distribution channel members to perform. The round the clock accessibility is extremely important especially in international trade where business is conducted across different time zones.

The global exposure is particularly desirable for tourism destinations which up until the mid-1990s had to depend entirely on promotion agencies in tourist generating regions to market its products. The Web has enabled tourism destinations to market themselves with well constructed and well promoted web sites. Furthermore, the Web facilitates doing business overseas by avoiding regulations and restrictions that companies must follow when they are physically present in other countries, for instance in many countries, foreign travel companies are forbidden from organising or selling tours. Finally, compared with the traditional media, the Web not only provides virtually unlimited access for hundreds of million users but also delivers unlimited amount of information on the Web as there is practically no restrictions in terms of the "space of advertisement" - the number of pages a web site can accommodate or the "bytes" of data a online database can hold.

Service Improvements

The Web helps companies to improve service quality at all stages of customer interaction - pre-sale, during sale and after - sale. De and Mathew identified that the Web provides four tangible improvements in customer service: first, larger accessible choice set for customer since a web site can display a vast set of product options and service options; second, faster payment processing for customers - through automatic processing of cyber-cash or credit card charges; third, reduced delivery time for many products such as online software and music distribution; and fourth, easier, faster and greater availability of support literature, and more detailed and particularised help. In tourism the web-based distribution systems can satisfy consumer needs for easy access to transparent and easy to compare information on a wide variety of choices of destinations, holiday packages, flights, lodging and leisure services. They also provide immediate confirmation and speedy documentation of reservations providing a greater degree of flexibility and enabling prospective travellers to book at the "last minute".

Increasingly, tourists' satisfaction depends on the accuracy and relevance of tourism information as well as the promptness of responding to consumers' requests. As a Delta Airlines executive said: "Most people will tolerate misconnects and changes when they occur in the airline industry what they won't tolerate is not getting timely and accurate information. The airline business today is much more than a transportation business. Many airlines are using the Internet, especially through mobile phones, to provide aggregate information in real-time to business partners, employees as well as customers. Across the tourism industry, the improved access to information covering all aspects of tourist activities has provided marketers with the opportunity to offer personalised services at price levels comparable to those of standard packages.

Cost Savings

The cost saving effect of the Internet derives mainly from five areas. First, the streamlining and electronic processing of booking and payments cuts down sales cost. Second, automation and the deskilling of tasks reduce the labour intensity and staff training cost. For example, the web-based travel reservation systems are much easier to use than the traditional viewdata systems. Third, by offering direct links between the producer and the consumer, the Net helps the producer to save huge distribution costs through the disintermediation process. Fourth, the ability of the Net in narrowcasting and electronic communication leads substantial savings on promotion in both "above and below the line" costs. Finally, cost savings in the form of reduced office and sales space, furniture and decoration outlay, and administration overheads.

The cost of setting up a promotional web site is relatively low. An average computer user, given a proper software package, such as Microsoft FrontPage can build a basic company web site in days. The marginal cost of adding an extra web-page to the site is negligible. The more comprehensive and powerful web-sites, such as a destination site offers complete information, a tour operator site with a virtual multimedia brochure to include thousands of product offerings, and a site which integrates information, reservation and transactions, will cost more and take longer to develop. However, compared with the tens of millions of dollars spent by airlines, tour operators and hotel chains on TV and magazine ads, the Web is a low cost medium for promotion. The simple web-presence, by providing information on the Net, and allow customers to find answers to their inquiries themselves can also help to reduce telephone charges based on toll-free numbers.

The Internet has also great potential for saving distribution costs. Distribution, the selling and marketing of tickets, is one of the biggest cost items in the airline industry. At British Airways, for example, distribution accounts for about 18% of its total costs of £8.5bn and a share of about 20 per cent is typical among big carriers. The chief executive of Swissair sees that the Internet can potentially save 50% of the airlines distribution cost. Airlines web-based ticket sale operation can at least eliminate the key distribution costs of an airline seat - travel agent commission and GDS fees US$3.20 gross. Internet-based supply-channel management can also save procurement costs for businesses. British Airways aims to increase the share of online purchasing from the current 25% to 80% in two years time and achieve a estimated saving of more than 5% of its annual £3.5 billion purchasing budget.

INTERNET APPLICATION IN HOSPITALITY INDUSTRY

Although applicable in all business activities, e-business has had the biggest success in the following areas until today:

— e-business
— e-marketing
— e-banking
— e-stock exchange
— e-reservation systems

In the first place, it is necessary to define the difference between the Internet and the World Wide WEB. The Internet is a huge data network that spans most of the globe, linked by an enormous assortment of high-capacity data cables, over thousands of routing locations. Data that travels over the Internet get broken into small pieces, or packets, which get routed to their destination and then reassembled.

Since the majority of given activities make an unavoidable component of doing business in the hospitality industry, it is possible to draw a parallel between traditional way of doing business and on-line way by using the Internet. The latter is becon ung increasingly competitive in terms of:

— providing information
— immediate contact with key service providers,
— immediate feedback to the given information,
— pricing,
— marketing and brand building,
— market research,
— booking / reservation.

However, using the on-line way does not exclude the traditional way, but enables expanding of the group of `old' customers, by reaching new on-line customers and establishing a whole new customer base. Also, UNCTAD, sugestes that new e-tourism channels should be integrated into traditional and non-traditional distribution channels and foster the development of special-interest tourism WEBsites. Therefore, conducting awareness campings about etourism is a special tasks for the hospitality industry.

WWW as Marketing Tool

Using the WWW for promotion and distribution of tourism products or services to potential consumers became inevitable. The Internet is a medium with the fastest increase of usage and it represents a new dimension in the promotion system in the global market. At the same tinge it is an effective system for competition which enables possibilities to use this direct distribution channel effectively. Tourism and tourism products are ideal for marketing on the Internet, because tourism is an information-intensive industry.

Internet develops a relationship of suppliers and consumers providing them with personalised promotional materials. Tourism organization can no longer be content to print brochures and catalogues, but it should fiinction by using uniovative range of techniques. Under these new circumstances, traditional marketspace model is broadened by two new elements:

1) Customer Relationships,
2) Technology dimension consisting of two separate elements

— interactivity, and

— connectivity.

Since the customer holding a central position within the marketspace is the priority, the creation of WEB sites must be directed towards him. Customer relationships are located in the central part of the marketspace model, and they point to an individual customer related marketing. There is also a growing realisation among corporations that the Internet has forever charred the traditional paradigm of marketing and remote customer contact.

The days of mass marketing and remote customer contact are gone. Interactivity designates intense relationships between an enterprise and customers, and creates new paradigms for product design and customer service. Connectivity refers to creation of a shared global marketplace.

The radical growth of connectivity is giving rise to new conunununication and coordination mechanisms linking organisations to their customers, as well as fostering greater communication between the customers themselves. In order to achieve the most effective connectivity, the WEB sites must be provided with the following links:

a) links leading from a selected destination to diverse offer items (including for example: accommodation, heritage, restaurants, events etc.),

b) links from already selected WEB site to other checked offer items within the destination.

In this way the service provider leads the WEB customer through diversified offer within this destination by recommending checked links on his own WEB site. Therefore, the WEB site of tourism enterprise has the effect of a marketing tool of both its own service or product and of the service or products of all other through links promoted enterprises.

Internet as support of Transactions

One of the major uses of the Internet is the development of Intemet-based reservation systems. They date back to the period when they were primarily used by air-line companies, but aflerwards they were transformed into multi-users systems without which it would be impossible for other transport companies, travel and hospitality organizations to function.

The enterprises in the hospitality indsutry have got two possibilities - either to use some of electronic advertisers of supply and demand as a means of sale and reservation of the services or to stay oriented only to the WEB site. In the both mentioned cases the WEB site is a means of both promotion and reservation.

While developing and implementing WEB reservation concept, the hospitality industry can use enormous advantages over the traditional reservation chaimels. In this way it has a possibility to offer automated payment, immediate access to valid price and availability of current information. In addition, this means reduction of steps a customer has to undertake while booking in traditional way, and consequently significant cost saving. The Internet also takes supportive role in conducting all transactions, some of them being: information, reservation, booking, payments, etc.

Today, the acceptance of this new model of reservation in the hospitality industry is increasing. Out of the total number of WEB sites, which was estimated 116.000 in 1999, according to some authors' assertions only 6%, i.e. 6500 offered the ability to execute transactions online.

It is already estimated that by year 2003 over 30% of online sales will be generated by on-line travel alone, including actual travel products as well as advertising earned by travel-oriented sites. UNCTAD sugestes that in order to build trust and consumer confidence and to ensure privacy and the protection of consumers and intellectual property rights, appropriate laws and regulations and service standards should be established. Moreover, hospitality industry employees should cooperate in setting up an international framework to protect travellers conducting transactions on the Internet.

Internet as Market Research Tool

In order to gain competitive position in the tourism market it is indisputable that Internet-based market research is necessary for finding the ways of adapting to the needs of on-line tourism service users. However, in contrast to traditional market reserach, if using the Internet as a medium for research, there is a possibility to get high qulity infomnation, with less costs and quite fast.

UNCTAD suggests that available research on e-commerce should be reviewed, and additional research conducted when necessary, in order to provide information on market trends, consumer needs, WEBsite use, demographic profiles and the impact of non-availability of on-line payments and other information that may support the development of a sustainable hospitality industry. A possible classification of internet based reserach is based on respodent's point of view' and is as follows:

1. *E-mail survey* - this is the oldest and the simpliest way of conducting research; a parallel to traditional mail surveys can be drawn.
2. *News-groups survey* - this kind of reserach is based on sin ular topic entities on the basis of which the reserach is being conducted and having as a consequence relatively small sample size.
3. *WEB based survey* - this is the most corrnrron way of the three. It represents a tremendeous potential for the market reserach experts, offering them a tool for fast and cheap reserach, generating more accurate information.

A prerequisite for a quality based research are high quality standards including sophisticated probability sampling, precise project control, rigorous quality control procedures, advanced questionnaire programming, and insightful analysis. Since WEB based surveys represent a growing segment of Internet research, the benefits of conducting them should be mentioned as divided in four different categories according to their characteristics:

1) inexpensive,
2) response speed,
3) overall effectiveness, and
4) its visual appeal.

However, certain problems should be taken into consideration. Dahlen, divides them in five categories:

1) self-selection,
2) unequal probabilities of sample inclusion,
3) unknown response rate,
4) not being noticed by people and
5) unnecessarily low response rates.

Although still in phase of development, WEB surveys are becornalg increasingly used by many tourism enterprises as significant tool for conducting market research. In a broader context, the technological improvement will affect the percentage of the population using the Internet. This will directly lead to the possibilitiy to sample the general population. All of thus will enable broad applicability of Internet research i11 the hospitality industry.

Email Marketing Strategy

Email marketing is a crucial component of the hotel eMarketing and online distribution strategy. The shift toward online purchasing suggests that the website is becoming a key point of entry to establish interactive relationship with your customers and capture client email profiles. Over 192 million North Americans are active Internet users (Nielsen) and 37 million of them have already purchased travel online. The Internet offers a vast, interactive, content-rich media and most importantly, a growing distribution channel for the hospitality market. It is estimated that 8%-10% of all hotel bookings will originate on the Internet in 2002. In fact, some hotels already generate 20%-30% of their total bookings from the Internet.

Email gets the most attention of any hospitality eMarketing effort because intuitively it makes sense—since email can create direct revenue opportunities with past, present, and future customers. Email marketing increases revenue opportunities throughout each customer's purchasing life cycle. The reason this is effective is because a total email marketing strategy addresses the entire buying process from initial email capture to message evaluation and everything in between including copy creation, type of messaging, follow-up, and vendor partnership, all components of a comprehensive communications strategy Once the strategy is built, an effective email campaign serves as a powerful sales force and marketing channel.

Why a total email marketing strategy in hospitality makes competitive sense:

— Serves both as direct-response vehicle and branding tool

— Creates personalized interactive relationships with customers

— Targets and entices recipients with relevant promotions

— Plants seed in the minds of recipients regarding future travel plans

— Serves as a tool to move distressed inventory

— Functions as a sales force – tens of thousands reached in seconds

— Recruits and retains customers, new and old

— Least expensive form of active marketing available

Today, everyone uses email. We read, forward, file, and print email. We send email to friends, family, and clients. Furthermore, almost everybody has at one time or another actively signed up to receive travel related information from a travel supplier or third-party collection service. Travel is a sought after product and a top information category chosen by most Internet users.

The Aberdeen Group indicates that email marketing has grown more than 270% from 1999 to 2000 and rapid growth is expected to continue well into 2005. An estimated 30 billion permission-based email messages were sent in 2001; a number that will grow to 150 billion in 2005.

By category, travel related email marketing retains a loyal audience, especially if it offers the recipient value, accurate communication, relevance, and familiarity. Forrester Research points out that on average, only 5 percent of recipients have ever unsubscribed from any travel related list. Indeed, some travel-related email campaigns report response rates as high as 25%. Let's face it; consumers want to learn about travel specials and promotions. Even travel agents serve as a viable audience as they too seek bookable opportunities.

Thanks to technology and the law, filtering agents and anti-spam laws have begun reigning-in annoying junk email. Filtering products such as Spamex and Spamcop, which cost less than $30 off the shelf, delete messages sent by anonymous senders to group lists and can filter by key words in the message itself.

Permission-based and Precision email marketing

Permission-based email marketing is the second-generation email approach that goes well beyond guerilla email marketing, known as email spam. A permission-based customer list is one in which you asked the customer permission to enter personal information voluntarily including an email address for the purpose of marketing, i.e. you obtain "permission" to send promotional emails. Opt-in or opt-out options enable the user to sign up or be removed from a marketing list. Growth in permission-based, 100% opt-in, opt-out practices consistently cleanse the customer lists to produce the most robust client lists possible. Once a firm starts an email collection process, it should include these features resulting in email that will be opened and read time and again without concern of violating email privacy norms.

Precision e-mail marketing is the next, third generation email approach that dynamically "reads" customer profiles, purchasing habits and history to create highly personalized emails. Over the past year airlines have used this type of marketing extensively to promote special offers in order to sell seats. Actually, permission based email and precision email marketing have become the airlines' preferred marketing tool. Why? It is cheap and it works! For example, precision e-mail marketing has generated up to a fivefold increase in response rates and tenfold lower conversion costs than direct mail (IMT Strategies).

Why does email marketing make sense for hoteliers?

— *Low cost*: Email is relatively inexpensive, pennies per email compared to $1 to $3 or more per direct mail.

— *Reach:* Almost instant outreach to an expansive client base, one email blast can be equivalent to thousands of sales calls.

— *Protects brand integrity:* Enables promotion of the latest specials on a one-to-one basis to a pre-selected audience without announcing to the world the latest discounts.

— *Personalization*: The recipient thinks this is a personalized invitation at a preferred customer rate.

— *Instant gratification*: People are at their computers most of the day and can receive, respond, forward, and print email almost immediately.

— *Rich Media*: Email marketing comes in various styles: text, e-Newsletters, HTML messages like a postcard or survey. The hotel gets its message across with sound, color, animation, video, whatever is most appropriate.

— *Results*: Outcomes based, from knowing who opened the message, clicked on which links, how much time spent viewing each page, completed a transaction, or forwarded the email.

Email for distressed inventory

Group cancellations and overestimations can make empty rooms the biggest competitor. It is well-known that the September 11th tragedy left hotels scrambling for solutions. Using email to move distressed inventory is an effective, practical option. With a well-executed message matched with a robust customer list, an email campaign can begin producing revenues within 24 hours without weakening brand integrity. The challenge is in collecting the right data and stratifying the data list to meet campaign objectives.

A Las Vegas hotel casino blasted an email promotion to an existing customer base. The message included a video insert and link to the booking engine.

The hotel experienced a 30% boost in occupancy within 12 hours of the campaign.

An Orlando hotel blasted an email promotion that included room nights combined with local attractions. The hotel included a "Forward to Friend" button that expanded the initial database. The campaign helped the hotel generate some 40% of total bookings online during that test month.

Customers for Email Marketing

This is an important question. There are three main groups of email audiences:

— consumers (leisure or business),

— travel intermediaries (travel agents, wholesalers) and

— corporate clients.

If a significant percentage of reservations come from transient business travelers, or from overseas tour operators, build campaigns that focus on these client segments.

Hoteliers can either buy a broadcast to a permission-based consumer email list from any number of third-party vendors or create their own "home-grown" email capture strategy, or do both. Renting from a third-party is an efficient short-term strategy. It creates an immediate audience and serves as a supplement to your own customer email database. Long-term, starting immediately, it is important to build an in-house customer database as part of a total email strategy. It is critical to capture client data at the property-level for the purpose of creating highly relevant, targeted email marketing campaigns.

Hoteliers are in a unique position to build a robust list from existing customers. Using a list built from existing customers, the conversion rates can be ten times greater than any standalone rented mailing list because the targeted group already knows and has experienced the product first-hand. In addition, the hotel can stratify the customer list by specific characteristics, communicate and offer value in the message, and send targeted and relevant mailings frequently to the intended audience, an audience that even anticipates these messages announcing hotel specials.

Hoteliers should carefully consider how large and comprehensive a customer list would be from a home grown collection strategy. Anyone who has stayed, inquired, or visited the property, visited the hotel website, or spoken to a receptionist by phone or in person qualifies. An organically grown database of customers can exceed the value of any customer list worth renting.

Reasons for building a homegrown customer list:

— Represents an existing client base

— Serves as a tool to access greater audiences, i.e. friends, family, colleagues

— Builds retention and overall loyalty

— Ownership of the database

— Low cost

Where can customer information be captured? The short answer is at any perceivable point of contact with customers: in the reservations process, on the website, through convention attendee lists, holiday parties, weddings, special events, at the front desk from walk-in customers, phone inquiries, groups and tour operators, travel agents and vendors.

How big is the potential homegrown customer email list? A U.S. hotel with 200 rooms has an occupancy rate of 62%. The average number of adult guests per room is 1.3 and the average stay is for 2 days for either business or leisure. The total number of guests for the one-year period would be 29,383 guests. If 60% of them use the Internet, the customer email list could be 17,630 strong within 12 months. A smartly done email broadcast to the entire list could produce a 5%-10% response rate, i.e. a minimum of 882 people will click a URL link in the email and come to the hotel website to see a Web-only special or promotion. Experiences show that 3%-5% of these qualified respondents will book i.e. minimum 26-35 people, which represents revenue of $4,420-$5,652 based on 1.9 night average stay and $85 per night ADR.

Does the website offer customer email capture functionality? If so, that website might draw 10,000 visitors per month, if optimized for the search engines. A conservative look to book ratio of 20:1 yields 500 transactions per month. Consider another 5% will sign up for promotions but not book producing, another 500 registrations. The total number annualized from the website could result in an estimated 12,000 new client profiles added to the database.

How does a hotel compare to today's average where 8%-10% of all revenues in hospitality are generated from the Internet? It is estimated that four years from now the Internet will contribute over 18% of all hotel bookings. Hoteliers are beginning to like what they see as online distribution cuts costs, attracts affluent customers and lessens the dependency on more traditional and expensive distribution channels. Hotels must employ new strategies to take advantage of these opportunities to capture this Internet market.

Travel Agent in Email Marketing

Why do travel agents represent such an important group for email marketing? Travel agents that use the Internet and email are exactly the travel agents hoteliers must reach. These agents are likely to visit hotel websites, book online, and even boast hotel web-only promotions in their own marketing efforts to preferred clients. Research from the most respected travel organizations, such as ARC, ASTA, IATA and Plog Research, as well as leading travel industry trade publications shows that:

— 96 percent of agents send and receive e-mail

— 79 percent of agents receive e-mail travel requests from clients

— 54 percent of agents e-mail clients with special offers or incentives

In the aftermath of September 11th, many New York City hoteliers teamed up to create joint marketing campaigns. Two notable campaigns were the popular "America Loves NY" and "This Week's Top Hotel Deals in NY", produced by Hospitality eBusiness Strategies. These HTML email campaigns ran on a weekly basis over the course of 6 months and provided links back to the hotel websites.

Data to collection

Collecting the right information is essential to not confuse long-term marketing plans. For example, in selling automobiles, single males and females have their own particular tastes and needs as do families and seniors. By asking the right set of questions on the website and at the front desk, the dealer can stratify his database to reach discrete audiences with the appropriate set of messages. It is essential to consider which audiences the hotel wants to reach and with what types of messages.

Based on the type of hotel and other variables, one can begin to get an idea of what data is important to build a customer database. It is critical to avoid the 9-deadly sins of email marketing and not appear anxious or aggressive when collecting client information. The hotel must collect with sensitivity resulting in a process that runs on autopilot whether it's online or through your reservation desk. Start collecting the data!

It is important to follow the path of the customer! Exploit every point of entry from the reception desk and corporate sales office, to the reservation operator and website. Create an environment suitable for data collection; client profiles from call-ins, walk-ins, or online lookers regardless if they are patrons, travel agents, or others. At the same time, a central repository will be helpful to avoid repeat inquiries from the same customers.

The hotels should always seek permission. It's been shown that if a hotel asks permission and clearly demonstrates how one can opt-in or out easily and conveniently, chances are the user will sign up and remain a loyal recipient of hotel emails. Such collection tactics include:

— Sign our "Guest Book"

— Announce a drawing

— Offer a promotion or special discount

— Refer a friend

— Follow up e-Questionnaire

— eSurvey

Outsourcing the technology support for email marketing makes complete sense. In 2001, an estimated 72% of all email campaigns were outsourced. Third-party vendors or "service bureaus" are inexpensive and this is their core competency. These vendors specialize in email messaging including email capture, hosting, managing, stratifying, blasting, and reporting outcomes of the campaign.

There are a plethora of third-party vendors ready to serve technology needs and act as guardian of the data. These low cost highly competitive ASP technologists want hotel business and can provide, at minimal cost, features and formats to capture, create, and blast a campaign. Some vendors offer templates to help design an eNewsletter while others support Macro Media for Flash. Hotels should understand the level of customer service each vendor offers. Of course, stick to your budget.

Not surprisingly some online booking technology vendors offer email collection and messaging management. Two are iHotelier and SecureRez, each with their own suite of tools to help a hotel build a total email marketing strategy.

A reputable service bureau adheres to the strictest rules permitted by law and will maintain client information in a secure environment. They will not rent or barter information to outsiders. However, hoteliers should seek advice on vendor selection, review of campaign, and vendor agreement.

Creating an E-mail Campaign

There are a number of guides to email marketing, starting with the marketing objectives? For example, is it to use email as a direct response vehicle? Or as a branding tool? Begin by devising a strategy, and start with these basic questions:

— Who is the target audience?

— How often should a hotel launch this campaign?

— Who will support the campaign?

— What is the budget?

A Canadian golf and spa resort generates a seasonal eNewsletter and sells advertising space on the mailing to local hiking, fishing, and boating clubs. As a conference-housing center, the resort hosts a high volume of business people who return for holiday. Some 7,500 patrons receive eNewsletters each season and the cost of the campaign pays for itself with the advertising from local vendors.

Email marketing is used for a range of purposes. What is the purpose of the campaign? According to Forrester Research these campaigns are used for the following:

— Promotion or discount – 66%

— Newsletter – 48%

— Product announcement – 34%

— Advertising/Marketing – 28%

— Alerts/Reminders – 24%

— Market Research – 8%

— Other – 4%

A quality email campaign delivers comfortable, interesting content, and offers value in the form of premiums, discounts, or specials. Whenever possible, the hotel should avoid the hard sell, be brief and to the point and never overstate the message.

A quality campaign would appear in an HTML newsletter. Today's browsers support viewing many forms of inviting eNewsletters. Information delivered in this fashion reinforces the hotel brand—its logo and colors—and organizes the delivery of content so that a quick glance may be all that's necessary to draw the user to link to a hotel website and book now.

Other suggestions include the need to clearly identify the hotel and intent in the subject line and property insignia. In addition, subject line must be relevant and personalized, if possible. The subject line should not exceed 80 characters.

Recent trends in email technology and services include:

— Built-in templates that incorporate hotel brand and insignia for on-demand email blast campaigns

— Dynamic content merge to produce highly targeted and timely campaigns (precision email marketing)

— Email forwarding features to increase client database collection and evaluate the campaign

— Multi-part MIME detects a users email box to discern AOL from Outlook from Yahoo to Hotmail to Lotus Notes, etc to assure guaranteed delivery

— Enhanced personalization from subject line to initial salutation

— Enhanced tools to help stratify your database by demographics, zip code, country code, language preference, past patrons, or any combination or permutation

— Integration and use of Rich Media, Flash, and HTML

— Numerous and hungry low cost service bureaus willing to make a deal

Important issues to remember:

— *Establish interactive relationship with customers*: Turn e-mail into a preferred communications vehicle, enabling the hotel to stay in touch with customers 24/7, from virtually everywhere.

— *Frequency*: Create a schedule and stagger blasts over an appropriate time frame. Use it immediately and often for distressed inventory or less frequently for seasonal activities and travel planning.

— *Personalize and Relevance*: Address customers by first names and offer information relevant to lifestyle and demographics. Don't blast an AARP special rate to young families, etc. A relevant campaign is worth its weight in gold.

— *Permission-based*: Recipients must actively offer information after having requested it. This narrows the scope of emails one receives on a constant basis and reaches those active information seekers.

— *100% Opt-In and Opt-Out is a self-policing cleaning mechanism*: Make it easy for recipients to opt-in or opt-out and they'll choose to remain on the list. This self-policing method allows the system to scrub and refine customer lists.

Needs of email users

A list of email users' opinions regarding ways permission marketers can improve their email programs, reported by a recent US survey report is given below:

42% - Less frequent messages

35% - Better prices and offers

24% - More relevant, targeted messages

18% - More Control over email options

18% - Time savers and convenience

17% - Exclusive e-mail offers .

A total email strategy addresses every aspect of the email marketing process. It's organized to leverage a hotel's existing and future client base for ongoing and upselling opportunities. This includes matching the right messages with the intended audiences for ongoing customer relations. In conclusion, a total email marketing strategy serves as a springboard to launch various email campaigns, to boost ongoing customer acquisition, relationship management, and increased bookings on and off line.

Website for Competitiveness in Hospitality Industry

The hospitality industry activities presented on the Internet have many advantages, but one should not underrestimate possible disadvantages this new medium might cause. Many authors are trying to determine advantages and disadvantages from doing business over the Internet. Benefits or competitive advantages of using the Internet in the hospitality industry are:

1) Service improvements concerning:

— large choice of access to a WEB site

— faster payment processing

— reduced delivery time for many products

— faster and greater availability of support literature

— more detailed and particularised

2) Low costs of:

— marketing

— processing of booking and payments

— automation of tasks

— establishing direct links between the producer and the consumer

— distribution

3) Differentiation from competition:

— creating, presenting and selling high-quality, distinctive products

4) Creating up-to-date enterprise image

5) Information usage including the following concepts:

— addressability

— interactivity

— flexibility

— accessibility

6) Efficiency i11 operational management and communication

7) Obtain know-how through discussion with news groups on the Internet

Potential disadvantages or threats of Internet usage in the hospitality industry are:

1) Characteristics of tourism product and services as being fragmented and difficult to evaluate
2) Standardization of legal procedures of doing business over the Internet
3) The problem of inefficient accessability to the WEB site/unfavourable indexing by search engines
4) Bad quality of individual WEB sites which might damage whole destination image
5) Nonprofessional detennination of purpose the WEB site is supposed to fulfil.

Great competitiveness in the hospitality industry bears enormous challenge for economic development and determines its perfonnance in the global market. The dominant key in achieving success in e-business and consequently competitive position is the quality which can be obtained only by using the Internet as one of the leading instruments of achieving (Total Quality Management), TQM.

Effective WEB site

Today there is a great amount and many kinds of tourism WEB sites from different tourism sectors, all of which have different purposes and thus providing different kinds of information The fast growth of travel and tourism information on this new medium is caused by customers' demand for higher service levels, better quality of information and tendency to book shorter vacations and to travel more spontaneous.

"The WEB is a vast sea of information. The user can access immense amounts of travel-related information, but the sites that provide information about a destination are very badly organised, the information is distrubuted and unstructured. To the traveller seeking for reliable information to plan a trip, the WEB is becoming more and more a time consuming horror where one gets easily lost.

Thus, a good site that serves as a useful tool to plan a trip has to overcome these limitations." Research on tourism WEB sites have started emphasizing the importance of creating effective WEB sites. However, research on the effectiveness of tourism WEB sites are not being conducted sufficiently. In addition, most of them were conducted on the basis of content analysis.

Today, some new cretaria about features and values of WEB sites have been established. The most important features of a WEB site are considered as:

— Being visually/graphically attractive,

— Providing correct and up-to-date infomlation,

— Being interactive,

— Enabling chat lines and stimulating consumer comments,

— Providing availability and booking online,

— Developing the right promotion online to entice the transient guest by providing attractive offers and interactive tools and using banners for brand image-building ,

— Capturing data for conducting direct e-mail campaignes. Retail databases are built with names and addresses of customers and prospect who visit the sites and inquire about fiuther infonnation.

There are several ways of measuring the effectiveness of tourism WEB site. According to a classification WEB sites may be measured from the perspective of content, content quality and design. Effective content is the one having purpose and bearing features which provide visitors with significant value. The former, in terms of quality, should have useful, informative, accurate, up-to-date and comprehensive content. Design, as the last issue in determining a WEB site as effective, means that the site is intuitive, easy to navigate and use, consistent, accessible, appropriate, interesting, fast and ftin.

Other possible methods are based on measuring the success of tourism WEB sites by the number of visits, viewings, clicks, inquiries, bookings and purchases. In addition, Rita claims that "successful sites are designed around the wants and needs of the targeted audiences." As effective a WEB site may be proclaimed if it is in line with its corporate strategy and this is considered to be another possible and interesting measurement of effectiveness.

Due to enormous meaning of information, especially of information quality within the WEB pages, it is necessary to mention the characteristics of good information, and these are: objectivity, completeness and pluralism. Also the UNCTAD covers this issue suggesting that enterprises should create and continually update local content on the Internet in local languages and languages of the most important tourism consumers in order to provide information and databases on tourism experiences and attractions and general information about destinations.

NET-BASED TOURISM MARKETING

Travel and tourism products are ideal for marketing on the Internet. This is because tourism is an information-intensive industry and the Internet is the most effective and efficient means in information exchange worldwide. The Net can greatly facilitate the promotion and distribution of tourist products and potentially enable tourism destinations and enterprises to compete on a level playing field.

Tourism Is an Information-Intensive Industry

Tourism is very information-intensive and information is often dubbed the "life-blood" or "cement" of the industry which holds together the different producers within the travel industry - airlines, tour operators, travel agencies, attractions, car rental, cruise lines, and other supplies. "In few other areas of activity are the generation, gathering, processing, application and communication of information as important for day-to-day operations as they are for the travel and tourism industry"

The perishability of tourism products and the often erratic tourist demand make the task of balancing tourism supply and demand far more significant than any other sector. That is probably why tourism became one of the first industries to widely apply IT and conduct electronic commerce from the 1960s in the form of computer(ised) reservation systems (CRSs) and then global distribution Systems (GDSs).

However, the traditional CRSs and GDSs had only improved the information communication between tourist businesses, originally between airlines and travel agents, as they do not directly interact with consumers.

The systems are also expensive to both the tourism producer and the retailer. For instance, the GDS cost accounted for an average 8.1% of the International Air Transport Association (IATA) member airlines' distribution cost in 1996, and the major GDSs charge around US$600 a month to put a terminal in a travel agency.

Moreover, the systems are flawed with incompatibility between each other, especially in the lodging sector, where "switch" companies such as THISCO (The Hotel Industry Switching Company) was needed to connect hotels with all the major GDSs to facilitate room reservations by travel agencies worldwide. With the effective use of the Internet, these problems can be addressed effectively and cheaply. In addition to its traditional function, a web-based GDS can increase the speed of information transmission, improve the quality of information delivery (from the old viewdata to the window-based computer screen), reduce the cost to the user as no special connections are necessary, and most important of all, has the potential to interact with all web users in the world.

Having realised the tremendous potential of the Internet, GDS companies already started to develop new and web-based systems which could transform the whole tourism distribution landscape in the near future. For example, Amadeus launched Amadeus Pro Web in January 2000, which is a browser-based reservation tool allowing travel agents to service customers worldwide without a dedicated communications line and at a greatly reduced cost. In fact, with this system any Internet user can become an online travel agent within a week.

Tourist Products and Services Are Difficult to Evaluate

As a service industry, most tourist products are intangible services, they are experienced and cannot be touched, tasted, smelt or seen and therefore difficult for tourists to grasp and evaluate. Furthermore, the spatial fixity of tourist attractions and amenities means that a tourist cannot really assess their quality until he arrives at the destination. Tourists have, for a long time, relied on limited information from holiday brochures and other literature to evaluate tours and destinations. Comprehensive, relevant, timely and accurate information is essential in tourists' holiday decision making process. But they were not readily available to tourists until the emergence of the Internet, especially the wide use of the Web.

With the Internet, virtually unlimited amount of information can be stored at a web site and an unlimited number of users can retrieve it at any time from anywhere in the world. The Web can not only provide more information but also provide it from a much wider range of sources; while in the past, tourists are almost exclusively dependent upon representations and descriptions by the travel trade.

The Web can also deliver the information in a greater variety of formats, from text to photos, graphs, audio and video clips, whereas in the past, tourists primarily relied on the printed brochures as the limited copies of videos of a limited number of tourism destinations or holidays were only available to the major travel agents. The web-based electronic brochure can also facilitate the complex process of choosing among the hundreds of holidays using browser-generated selections from back-end databases linked to web servers whereas the printed brochures are usually arranged and indexed by one way, often by destination.

Through Internet video telephony, tourists can also "test drive" a prospective holiday by viewing real-time scenes through cameras placed in hotels, clubs, restaurants, scenic spots and other sites in the destination and transmitted via the Internet. Video clips can also show episodes and scenes of festivals, art performances and service delivery to facilitate tourists in the comparison and evaluation of intangible services, the quality of which is otherwise difficult to assess in advance.

Tourism Distribution Has Travel Tickets to Deliver

Since in tourism, it is the tourists who travel to the destination, rather than the tourist product be transported to the market. When a tourist books an airline seat, a hotel room, or a package holiday, he acquires the right to use that seat, room or holiday in the specified time period. After the tourist completed his journey or holiday, he takes nothing home but experiences (though often together with some photos and souvenirs). In the whole process, from the booking, through the out journey to the return journey, the only things being transported are travel tickets and the tourist himself. This unique characteristic offers tourism a great advantage in Internet marketing as the only cost of online sale will be the transaction processing expense plus a little postage cost; in contrast, for manufactured goods, the delivery cost is often substantial.

With the increasing popularity of electronic-ticketing (e-ticketing) or ticketless-travel, especially among airlines, online tourism distribution over the Web may one day have no physical goods (not even a ticket) to deliver at all. Ticket-less travel means that check-in is achieved by proof of identity and a booking reference number. This saves the cost of ticketing for the airline which would usually include stationery, printing and postage and speeds up the check-in process at airports by enabling passengers to self check-in at check-in machines with a credit card.

Worldwide, there are more than 30 airlines offer e-ticketing in at least some routes in its networks. About 60% of United Airlines' passengers are now using c-tickets. British Airways has even announced that from May 2000 travellers will be charged £25 for a printed ticket where e-ticketing is available for the flight. It could also cost the traveller £50 to replace a lost paper ticket. Obviously, c-ticketing is a key development that will accelerate the acceptability and convenience of booking air travel via an on-line travel agent. Since such a web-based e-ticket seller has no physical ticket to deliver, it can potentially sell from anywhere in the world to anyone in the world.

Tourism Destination Product Is Fragmented

As a place product, tourism includes all the elements a destination has to offer to tourists, including the social, cultural and physical environments as well the "touristic" components of tourism supply such as attractions, transport and lodging facilities, and other travel related services. Pollock highlights the difficulties in tourism destination marketing which are attributable primarily to two factors.

First, tourism is fragmented in that while the tourist looks at a holiday as a complete "experience", it is sold in the market place "in bits" as beds, meals, tours, seats, etc. by a plethora of independent suppliers that operate independently of one another.

Second, no one agency controls or can deliver content about a destination's tourism product as the marketing of a tourism destination is shared by another plethora of organisations such as tourist information centres, regional tourism boards, national tourism organisations and national tourist offices overseas located in main generating markets.

The Internet provides the effective means for a destination to develop a sustainable electronic "infrastructure" that is capable of establishing a comprehensive and multi-lingual destination web site. This site can present existing and potential tourists with up to date information, from a variety of sources, about the destination in all aspects of tourism - tourist attractions, transportation, accommodation, tour operators, travel agencies, shopping and leisure facilities - as well as the background of its people, culture, history, economy, climate. The master destination database can be integrated through hyperlinks with individual tourism companies as well as with suite of applications which enable tourists to pick and mix to make their own holiday "packages".

As such a mega-site could be the "portal" or the "home page" of the web sites of all tourism enterprises in a destinations, it is a great deal easier for the destination to establish itself in the already crowded web-space. From this first stop-of-call, an visitor can search for all the information he needs to make a decision as to whether to visit the destination, what facilities to use and to arrange for reservations and transactions online. In comparison, with the traditional media, in order to get the relevant information of a destination a tourist often needs to go to a travel agency to get a brochure, to a bookshop to get a guide book, and may also contact the destination's national tourist office to get some promotional literature. Furthermore, the printed literature the tourists get is often outdated while a properly constructed and maintained web site can provide right-to-the-minute information.

Majority of Tourism Enterprises Are Small In Size

The fragmented tourism industry is also polarised in that on the one hand, there are a few large multinational airlines, tour operators, hotel chains and theme parks; on the other, there are millions of small and often family owned businesses, especially in the travel retailing, tour guiding, hotel and catering sectors. For example, in Scotland the average size of the accommodation establishment in the Bed and Breakfast sector was 2.5 rooms in 1999. For the small tourism enterprises, the Web is probably the first effective and feasible medium for them to carry out professional marketing function beyond the basic sales and operating activities.

The Internet has opened the door for small businesses with little capital to reach a worldwide market. Open access results in lower entry barriers so that virtually anyone can both access and provide content to the Internet. Travel retailing is one of the sectors m the economy that requires very little initial capital investment. The Net also re-defines economies of scale, allowing small firms to achieve low unit costs for products and services in markets (such as tour operating) dominated by large companies.

In the hospitality sector, small firms could also have more cost-effective marketing through the destination's web-site than the printed tourist directory. In essence, the Web "levels the playing field". For this reason, Inkpen goes so far as to praise the Internet as a marketer's "dream" because it enables companies of different sizes to compete on more equal terms. This analysis also applies to tourism destinations. For example, a strong web presence may substantially increase the exposure of many small and developing destinations in the Western market where the high cost of mass media advertising made such exposure practically impossible in the past. Nevertheless, it must be noted that although it costs little to achieve a web exposure, the development of a fully functional marketing and sales site and especially the promotion of the site to increase visitor numbers require huge investment.

Applications of Internet in Tourism Marketing

The Internet as a marketing media can be of great benefit to virtual all areas of marketing, from marketing research, through market segmentation, targeting and positioning, to the effective use of the marketing mix, and marketing organisation and control. The following discussion does not attempt to provide an exhaustive list of the Net's use in tourism; rather, it simply intends to exemplify its common applications in and main implications for tourism marketing.

Market Reserach

The Internet does more than automating online business transaction, it can "informate" in that it provides a vast amount of information which was previously unavailable. Marketing is essentially an information-processing activity which links an organisation to the external environment in which it operates. The Internet is an invaluable source of low cost but up-to-date marketing intelligence which can be sourced through a company's own site and other web sites. The Internet is extremely useful in build a customer information database. With the use of proper software such as Aurum Software's Web-Trak it is easy to gather systematic data about all users who visited the company's web site. This information can be used to identify prospects, understand customer needs and customise resources to give greater levels of service to customers. A database of online transaction histories can be the primary marketing resource of tourism companies, determining what kind of travel products they can deliver, what market segments they serve best, and what is the lifetime value of each customer to the firm.

By searching other web sites, a company can get valuable information about market demand, supply, competition and economic, demographic, legislation and technological changes in the domestic and international markets. Web sites of government agencies, media companies and non-profit organisations usually provide large amount of information free on general issues; while commercial sites are good sources of information on new technologies, best business practices, and industry initiatives.

Scanning competitors' home pages helps companies to track competitors' marketing strategies and tactics. For example, from hotel chains' web sites, one can easily locate information about the chains' main business activities, financial performance, new hotel openings and investment plans, and key marketing strategies; whereas airlines' web sites often show such useful data as business and financial analysis, strategic alliance groups, new routes development and fleet expansion plans, frequent flyer programmes and the fares and availability of flights between any two destinations.

Market Targeting

An important feature of the Web as a medium is that it is the consumer who is actively searching for information about products or brands in which they are interested. In effect the consumer is "pre-screened" and shows both interest and involvement in visiting the web site. While on the Web, the consumer can also provide instantaneous feedback to the marketer. All the feedback, and indeed, every "click" or "hit" the user makes can be memorised by the web server.

Through the application of the IT data mining technique, companies can find patterns within their internal customer data and make sense of data or turn data into meaningful marketing information. For instance, the visitation record of an online brochure may show the total number of hits, the distribution of the hits among the pages and across time, the order of the pages been accessed.

The user's visitation data can be easily combined with user profile information from user registrations through online visit cards or questionnaires and used to uncover the consumers 'interest and the patterns of demand and buying behaviour. This in turn leads to identification of likely target segments, often niches based on specific benefit sought. Armed with such information, organisations can refine their targets and develop specific means to achieve true one - to- one marketing.

The appropriate use of user profile and surfing behaviour data can improve the effectiveness and efficiency of market segmentation and targeting. This is because the traditional approach to market segmentation is often based simplistically on geographical, demographic and economic variables while the psycho, behavioural or lifestyle data is costly to collect and difficult to measure and compare.

In Internet marketing, it is easier to collect these data from potentially each and every user of the company web site, though tangible rewards such as free prize draws and free membership, are often needed to attract users to fill in web forms. It is even a great deal simpler and more effective in market targeting as the email messages and even tailor-made web-pages can reach the intended receiver with little cost. It is possible to set up 'virtual" or cyber - communities for each target market niche in the form of news-groups through which consumers with similar interest and behaviour patterns can be sent with relevant product offering and other information from the marketer. Members of such Internet communities can regularly exchange information between them and strengthen a sense of belonging.

Product

One of the major advantages of the Internet in marketing is that the tourist can here be a value creator for tourism companies through redefining the labour division between the marketer and the tourist in providing tourist experiences. This is because, on the one hand, tourists can provide individual preferences for or specifications of holiday packages through feedback in the forms of web forms, email messages or simply the 'clicking' patterns, which the tourism marketer can use to development new products or tailor-make existing products to suit the needs of particular consumer(s). In this sense, the Internet has accelerated a shift in the nature of products from mass produced and tangible to customised and information based.

On the other hand, the self-servicing tourist can not only conduct transactions online and reduce costs of sales for the supplier but also actively participate in the production process itself. Provided with choices, a tourist can now assemble his own product according to the specifications desired. This is especially useful in the production and marketing of package holidays. Tour operators, for example, can offer modular products or services, such as flights, rooms, tours, car hire and performances on their web sites, and allow the user to participate in the development of the specific holiday packages using a menu of options, ie., 'pick and mix" his own package.

As tour operators negotiate with the providers of these separate holiday items and buy in bulk, The economies of scale will enable the operators to offer lower "parts" prices to individual consumers than they buy directly from the different producers of the travel products. At the meantime, since the booking engine is integrated with the product inventory, it is easy for the operator to adjust in real-time the prices of different holiday components in response to their relative popularity and demand patterns.

In this way, tour operators can effectively provide the market with low cost and flexible (rather than the conventional rigid) package tours This is what both marketers and consumers have long dreamed for - high quality products made individually at a unit cost level of mass production -all enabled by the power of the Internet. Internet technologies can also contribute to the improvement of current products on offer or development of new products and services that redefine the company's strategic position. For instance, Boeing announced on 27 April 2000 plans for a network which will allow passengers to use the internet, watch TV and receive other data while flying.

Called Connexion by Boeing, it will use satellite technology to provide broadband services to aircraft, which could greatly improve passengers' flight experiences. The introduction of electronic ticketing (e-ticketing) and flight information exchange through mobile phones by many airlines in recent years also improve customer services. The Internet also give tourist attractions such as museums and galleries wider format options for electronic presentation and show web collections which are physically impossible to construct. Zoos and aquariums can improve its product offering through 'live" camera links using web sites like whale-watching to show views of animals not in captivity.

Pricing

The role of the Internet in pricing is based on its ability in processing and exchanging large amount of data instantaneously with a great number of people. This information processing capacity enables a company to analyze relevant pricing data effectively and quickly. The information exchange capacity enables firms to set and change prices in real time and also facilitates online bidding and flexible pricing. Both of these qualities of the Net are extremely useful in tourism marketing.

The major tour operators in the UK, for example, produce some 2,000 to 3,000 brochure pages annually, most pages feature a price panel with perhaps 100 separate prices, making a total of about a quarter of a million individual prices. The sheer number of prices, together with the fact that most brochures are launched 10 months in advance of the holiday season, mean that pricing in the travel industry is extremely difficult Since it is unpractical to set the prices for such a great number of holidays on the bases on demand analysis or competition research, most operators simply follow a cost-plus policy with little regard to the market changes in the months to follow. Even an operator wishes to adjust its holidays prices it is a costly and cumbersome process as new price panels have to be printed and distributed to the travel agencies.

With the help of a web-based reservation system, the task can be a great deal easier. A tour operator can make real-time adjustment to its thousands of holiday prices at a touch of a button in response to competition moves and demand changes. A special late-booking section can also be included in the main web site to promote 'left-over" holidays at the last minute to solve the problems of over-supply or under-demand in the package tour industry which has become a chronic issue in the UK during the last decade or so.

In Internet marketing, the potential for price discrimination is diminished given the enhanced capability of consumers to identity the least expensive source, regardless of supplier or location. The skilled consumer could have the "perfect knowledge" of market prices, which could facilitate the realization, to certain extent, of 'perfection competition" at the national and global markets. This will lead to the increasing standardisation of prices across companies or even borders, especially for the undifferentiated products such as airline seats, beach holidays and city breaks. Other applications of pricing on the Web including bidding and flexible pricing - many web-based businesses allow customers to bid for products on their sites.

Customers commit to the sale if the price is agreed upon. The bidding locks in customers to the sale and the committed price. This is a flexible pricing strategy where the buying capacity of the customer reflects in the eventual price. Companies such as Ebay.com and Bid.com have developed a model where other vendors can place products up for bids. Airlines could sell seats on over-demanded flights or routes through online bidding to the highest bidders to generate extra revenue.

Tour operators may use online bidding in a different manner to market special holidays the demand for which may be extremely difficult to estimate in advance. For example, a tour operator can put on its web site the details of a package holiday to the moon and the total cost (including profit margins) for a group, say 50 travellers, the more people bid the lower the price for each traveller. This way of pricing could well enhance the operator's image and profitability, as it is both an innovative marketing and sound financial approach.

Place

The uniqueness of the Internet as a means of distribution is based on the fact that it exists in "cyberspace" thus physical phenomena such as location and distance are less significant or even irrelevant. For the producer, the Web enables it to have direct links with consumers at a low cost therefore provides it with the opportunity of "disintermediation". For the retailer, the Web threatens its livelihood and changes its critical success factor from location, location, location to access, access, access. For the wholesaler, web-based business means it can bypass retailers while at the same time risk being bypassed by the producers.

The foremost role of the Web in tourism distribution is the direct electronic reservation and transactions between tourism product supplier and consumers. Aldridge et al argues that direct marketing is the name of the game on the Internet, offering both consumers and marketers greater control and lower potential costs of access due to the conveniences of the Net.

Because direct channels may be producer-direct or intermediary-direct, the potential for channel conflict will be magnified. In order to assuage channel conflict and price competition between direct-sellers and retailers, both producers and intermediaries will have to develop augmented product features and unique benefits. For example, direct online booking of airline tickets often carries special benefits not available from travel agents, such as extra frequent-flyer miles; while purchasing an airline ticket from an online travel agency may also benefit from such services as hotel reservations and travel insurance.

Airlines are among the first industry to invest in and develop CRSs and GDSs to exploit the potentials of IT. The Web offers the airlines even greater opportunities in streamlining and shortening the distribution channel. The no-frills or low-cost airlines emerged in the last few years are already heavily relying on the Web to distribute flight tickets directly to customers. The major global airlines have also started to believe that the Internet offers a unique opportunity to drive down costs and restore profitability to the sector which is troubled with financial losses across the globe. British Airways, for example, launched an e-business strategy recently which places the Internet at the centre of its efforts to transform relationships with both customers and suppliers. It is planning to invest £90 million during the next two years to develop its web-based operations with the aim of increasing the share of tickets sold over the Internet from less than 1% in 1999 to 50% by 2004. It is also preparing to operate via mobile phones and interactive television. Major airlines have also started to use the Internet to manage the supply channel and reduce procurement costs. For instance American Airlines, Air France, British Airways, Continental Airlines, Delta Airlines and United Airlines have agreed to jointly create and operate a web site that will handle supply purchases with US$32 billion a year.

The biggest change to tourism distribution brought by the Web could, in the next 5 to 10 years, be the noticeable shrinking of the travel agent sector. Agents are squeezed by both a decreasing market as more and more consumers go online and book directly from airlines and operators and by airlines' declining commission levels. The Association of British Travel Agents (ABTA) believes that the Internet will not cut out the middleman, but it will certainly put their added value under scrutiny. It warns that High Street travel agents that do not excel in what they do may not survive the competition. Nevertheless, the travel agent sector will not be doomed to extinction. How far and how soon the role of travel agent will diminish in the future is dependent upon how flexible and innovative the travel agents can be and how fast the Web can dominate both business and everyday life. The Travel agency will have to reinvent itself to suit the new Internet era by transforming from a travel ticket seller to a travel information manager.

For tour operators, the potential disintermediation has a dual effect. On the one hand, they can be bypassed by the producer as airlines and hotels that directly sell their products to the travel agencies and consumers; on the other, tour operators could benefit from its own direct sell operation by eliminating the travel retailers. It is hard to estimate the full impacts of the two. But one thing is sure to say that the tour operators, more than travel agencies, have a future in the Internet era. This is based on the understanding that tour operators are not purely intermediaries as they do perform some production function in assembling the various parts of tourism products into a marketable package.

Through this value-creating activities, tour operators can provide convenience and better value for consumers, by passing on to them some cost savings gained through bulk buying the separate components of the package, than they would otherwise get from the individual tourist product providers. The major tour operators are also 'backward" integrated and have their own charter airlines thus major schedule airlines' direct selling is not much as a threat to them as to travel agents.

Promotion

Arguably, the component of the marketing mix being most quickly transformed as a result of Internet usage is promotion. The Internet provides a labour-efficient and cost-effective way of distributing information almost instantaneously to millions of potential clients in the global markets. Internet promotion combines mass media's reach with the personalization inherent in two-way dialogue -previously only possible in personal selling. It can be used for corporate visibility, brand name recognition, advertising, public relations, corporate sponsorship, direct sales, sales promotion, customer support and technical assistance. There are three main issues in the application of the Internet to tourism promotion.

First, present the promotional information on the company's web site. The Web enables more information to be transmitted to (potentially) more people cheaply, instantly and with multimedia effect. The key to achieve these benefits is a well-designed and maintained web site which is attractive, informative and interactive. Through its multimedia capability, a good web site can and should incorporate information as accurate and detailed as brochures or timetables, photos and graphs as glossy as magazine ads, and videos as entertaining as TV commercials. The site can and supply as much promotional information as possible as there is virtually no capacity constraints or advertising space limits on the Web. By hyper-'inking pages together in an appropriate fashion, the Web marketer can create an ultra-comprehensive brochure to include everything a user wishes to know. For instance, a tourism destination web site may become a 'information mall" which provides the users with all the basic information about it such as the exchange rates, local traditions, weather, what to buy, etc. and, through the hyperlinks to the sites of tourism firms, details of flight schedules, tour prices, park opening times, late offers, and so on. A company web site with email links or even telephone numbers and address will enable users to contact it for further and often more personalised information.

Second, promote the web site itself to increase its exposure and visitation since a company's web site has to compete in the clutter of thousands of other web sites selling similar products and services. This can be achieved through a number of ways. A memorable Internet address to help user locate it on the Web, usually the company or brand name or a catchy word or phrase. Links "from" other web sites, by registering with search engines and online directories and paying relevant sites for click-through links or banners ads, are particularly important if the company's site is not well known. Links 'to" other sites, such as those offer news or entertainment services and those offer complementary products can also make the site more interesting as well as providing more relevant and up-to-date information for the users. Promoting the web site through the traditional media is also important, especially when it was first set up. For example, expedia.co.uk launched a £4 million promotion campaign on British TV and Press recently. The company's web address should also be included on all its media messages "to drive consumers to the Web".

Third, use the company's web site as a platform for advertising sites or products of other businesses. Through "banners" and banner linked web pages, a company's web site can also generate revenues by becoming an advertising medium for other organisations. Indeed, the effectiveness of the Web as a medium for advertising has already made online advertising a boom business itself. The Internet Advertising Bureau's research shows that online advertising revenue reached US$4.62 billion in 1999. It also finds that banner advertisements is the predominate type of advertising, accounting for 56%, sponsorships at 27%, interstitials at 4%, email at 2%, and other rounding out the category at 11%. Increased Web advertising will reduce the attractiveness and spending on some traditional forms of promotion such as direct mail, outdoor displays and radio advertising. Fletcher Research predicted that the online advertising spending in the UK would soar from £50 million in 1999 to £625 million by 2004, while expenditures on direct mail could see a 33% fall in the same period.

Constraints on Internet Tourism Marketing

The Internet has created great opportunities for tourism marketing. However, the current level of online travel sales is low though most researchers expect it to increase rapidly in the next few years. For example, it was estimated that purchases of travel products represent just 6% of overall Internet sales and 0.5% of all travel and tourism spending. In the US, Jupiter Communications forecasts that online travel bookings will grow from US$2.2 billion in 1998 to US$ 16.6 billion by 2003, representing a market share of total travel sales of 1.7% and 9.6% respectively. In the UK, Thomas Cook predicts that one in five package holidays and 40% of all flights will be sold via the internet or digital television in the next three years. Obviously, the comparative advantages of using the Internet in tourism marketing is compelling but its full potential as a marketing tool will only be realised if a number of well-documented limitations are successfully addressed.

Demand Factors

Consumer demand is the fundamental determinant of all forms of businesses. Whether an industry is initially supply-led or demand-driven, consumers are the key force in deciding the scale, structure, style and speed of its development. The small size of Internet business transactions in the world economy at present is caused to a great extent by insufficient demand, though more limited by consumers' willingness than their ability to shop on the Net.

First, the penetration rate of computer using and Internet connections is still low worldwide. In the main developed countries, about 30-50% of the adult population are Internet users while the global average is about 1-2%. One estimate shows that in 1997, there were 50.2 million web-users, of which 60% were in US and 20% in Europe; the world total web-population in 2001 was predicted to be 174.5 million, the US and Europe account for 54% and 18% respectively.

Although people with Internet access tend to be more affluent, better educated and younger than the average consumer, the small number of web-population does reveal that globally it is still a relatively small market. Furthermore not all web-user are frequent users. In the UK for example, a quarter of the 15 million adults with Internet access surf the Web less than once a week, and only a fifth of web-users have actually ordered something via the Internet. At the well publicised travel web cite - lastminute.com - only 6% of its 1.5 million register users have ever purchased anything there.

Second, the low frequency of web surfing is mainly caused by high access cost, especially in countries outside of North America. In the UK for example, local telephone charges are still metered, though the Internet subscription fees has largely gone from last year. Most consumers find it is an expensive hobby to surf the Web, especially when the search task is complicated by low speed and difficulties in locating the desired information. The main

UK Internet service providers (ISPs) have recently launched unmetered packages which will be available from mid-2000. This new development could see a surge in web visitation in the country.

Third, The vast majority of users access web sites for information or entertainment purposes rather than for online shopping. Among the Net resources, email is the most frequently used, news and sports sites attract more visitors than commercial sites, and sex and MP3 are for many years the most searched key words. Although Internet transactions offer the potential benefits of convenience and cost savings, due to factors discussed later, consumers still believe traditional shopping methods are more reliable and sometimes more economical. A recent survey of 50,000 Internet users in the UK show that 80% used the Web to access email while less than a third had bought online.

Fourth, concerns over privacy, information abuse, web crime, payment security and undelivery or late delivery, are often cited as the main inhibitor to online shopping. There is a lot of trust involved in online shopping. A web users has to trust that he receives the product he orders as well as trust its quality to be as described. He also wants to be sure that his private information such as address and credit card numbers is handled sensitively. However, there is at present no special legal provision to protect consumers' interest in web transactions and according to a Consumers International survey: 6% of the items ordered took more than a month to arrive and at least 8% never did; many sites did not give clear information about delivery charges; only 13% of sites promised that they would not sell customers' personal information on to a third party; and only 53% of the companies had a policy on returning goods. As a result, in average less than 1% of those 'looking" are actually 'booking" at the web site.

A recent MORI survey of package holidaymakers in the UK also found that only 45% of the respondents answered 'Yes" to the question of "In principle (if you had access) would you be prepared to book a holiday through the Internet?" while 46% answered "No"; and 9% answered "Don't know". A report on travellers' use of the Internet in the US, which has the most advanced Internet businesses and Internet users, shows that 52.2 million people used the Internet for researching travel in 1999 but only 16.5 million (32%) of which actually made their travel reservations online.

Finally, consumers' anxiety over safety and security in online shopping is further exacerbated by frequent media reports about web security breaches and frauds, and insufficient knowledge of the matter itself. Most of the security worries are caused by people who are not sufficiently aware of the possible protection that exists. Although the Web is generally considered to be user friendly and even 'foolproof", a user without the proper IT knowledge and skills will certainly encounter more problems and feel less confident in conducting web-based transactions.

Technological Factors

Many of the current constraints and problems of conducting web-based business are caused by the Web technology itself. 'Web technologies consist of the hardware, software and networks that enable individuals and organisations to connect with and interact with the World Wide Web. Hardware consists of the client terminals, the server, the gateway, the router, and hubs.

The software consists of operating and application software, including the browsers and application software on the client side, database servers, web servers and other application servers on the server side, and network operating systems and managers on the network side. The networks consist of cables, either leased or proprietary, and message carrier services". The main causes for concern over the ability of the Web in implementing c-commerce are as follows:

The Web's slow speed, often dubbed as the 'world wide wait", slows down the growth of the web-based businesses as users are often not prepared to wait for too long to see the information appears on the screen. The slowness of the Web is a combined results of three factors: the increasing number of Internet users, the increasing frequency of use, and the increasing richness of the information being transferred over the Internet.

Technology will not reduce these growing demands on the Web, on the contrary, technology will constantly expand the Web's capacity for accommodate and even stimulate the increasing demand. For example, the new digital broadband service, due to be introduced in the UK this year, could offer instant and always-on high-speed Internet access. It will not only enable much faster Internet access but also enhance facilities such as interactive digital TV and video e-mail. The advent of broadband and mobile accessibility is creating a second wave in Internet development. Research shows that a broadband customer will stay online four times as long as a narrowband customer, and spend nearly three times as much on c-commerce.

Functionally, the Internet is close to fully operational for commercial purposes. The main remaining impediment to maximum use of the Internet for c-commerce is the concerns for information security. The securing of information includes the protection of:

(1) confidentiality -providing confidentiality in the transmission (and sometimes the storage) of data;

(2) authentication -proving the identification of the individuals both transmitting and receiving the data; certifying that all parties to a transaction are indeed who they claim to be; and

(3) non-repudiation - providing proof that the transaction actually took place, establishing an irrefutable time stamp on the sending and receiving of the message.

In particular, there is an urgent need for an integrated financial transaction system that is suitable for an open electronic marketplace such as the Internet. How the consumer will pay for goods and services and how the provider will receive the payment securely over the Internet are issues which are being seen as some of the most important success factors for Internet commerce. A survey of US corporations revealed that 75% of the executives lacked confidence in the Internet as a vehicle for electronic commerce, primarily because of the vulnerabilities. The risks in electronic commerce are shown in poor security such as: from the short-cuts in the software development process, shortcomings in the popular operating system, deficiencies in the Internet protocols and problems inherent in managing the Internet.

Related to security is the issue of 'cyber' crimes. Internet crimes include not only fraud and theft-related activities, which simply represented the extension of traditional crimes into the electronic environment, but also new and more advanced forms of abuse such as hacking and computer viruses.

Web scam and online credit card fraud are also increasing rapidly. Visa International says that half of all credit-card disputes are about Internet transactions, despite online transactions making up just 2% of Visa's overall business. Visa found that across the EU only 5% of consumers trust e-commerce. Web technology does not cause the web crimes but these cyber crimes are more difficult to prevent and detect as they are committed in a virtual space. Unless the IT industry can come up with some effective solutions to the security problems in web-commerce, consumers will have to either take a high risk in or stay away from Net-shopping.

Furthermore, the 'unorganised" nature of the Web, makes it difficult to locate the information users desired. The Web offers an uncontrolled and vast universe of information: there are now about 5 million web sites with some 1 billion web pages. However, there is no overriding structure and control over information, no single entry point to the Web, and no centralized directory of content. Although the development of search engines and online directories has made finding information somewhat simpler, it i~ still easy to get distracted or lost during a search and much precious time can be wasted in gathering information. Ironically, this may negate the productivity benefits that derived from its use.

The other problems of the Web can be seen from Internet Industry Almanac's "Top 10 pain in the Net" - junk email, slow web sites with too many images to load, web sites with white text that you can't print, cookies, broken links, interstitial ads, hard-to-read tiny text, web sites with no basic company information, old forgotten web sites, and the server is not responding.

Organisational Factors

The low level of web-based business is also attributable to the failure of business organisations in implementing the Web technologies in operation and marketing. Most business leaders did not realise the potential impacts of the Web on commerce until very recently. A survey of US hotel managers found that they believe the Internet will 'someday" become an effective marketing and communication tool but not at the present time. Ironically, respondents with greater exposure to the Net rated its present usefulness lower than those with no net experience. On the other hand, those same experienced users gave the Net's future prospects a much higher rating than the inexperienced respondents.

Many companies, even with recognition of the advantages of the Internet in marketing, failed to exploit its full potential due to the lack of management commitment, investment capital and the qualified technical and managerial personnel. This is particularly the case for small tourism businesses. In the UK for example, travel agents are not using the Internet to provide better service to customers because of perceived investment and access costs and fear of new technology. Sabre (UK) recently discovered that fewer than half of its agency customers had an email address.

On the other hand, some large travel corporations failed to develop web-based operations wholeheartedly due to both complacency about their market leader positions and the vested interest in their highly vertically integrated business structure. The top three tour operators in the UK - Thomson, Airtours and First Choice - for instance, did not have a formal Internet strategy until March 2000. They probably overlooked the potential of the new Internet start-ups since the Net-commerce had a slow start and the travel web sites were mainly selling airline seats instead of package tours. The major tour operators were also concerned with the impacts of web-based operation on their own travel agent chains because the "disintermediation" in travel distribution saves operator side cost at the expense of losing businesses at the agency side.

As a result, not all tourism companies are on the Web. When they are on the Web, most of their web sites are PR or promotion sites that provide merely the companies a presence on the Net or little more than advertisements for their products and services. With the few comprehensive sales and transactions web sites, users were often asked to phone an operator or offered a brochure in the post. Just a fifth of the UK's top 40 tour operators have a real-time booking facility on their Internet sites. A recent survey also shows that 62% of the travel companies which have facilities to sell via the Web or email have less than 1% of its total business is conducted through online booking.

Even when web sites are fully operational in real-time transactions, such as many airlines owned sites, they often offer limited choice. Consumers increasingly want to use the web, and they want the convenience to see all the options in one place, no matter which airlines or tour operator is involved. However, most of the travel products on sale over the Net are stored at various web sites owned and operated by individual companies, such as airlines, tour operators, travel agencies and ferry companies.

Another problem is that the Web does not always offer the lowest prices compared with the traditional distribution outlets. Research by Express Money shows that booking holidays and flights through the Internet is not cheaper and traditional, low-cost outlets offer lower prices for several popular destinations. This is particularly the case for airlines as where a single flight could have over 50 different fares, the cheapest fares are usually given to flight-brokers or consolidators. Since most web users consider 'price" as the most important factor in buying an airline ticket, they will certainly be discouraged from booking directly on the Web when they realise that the traditional agents offer better deals.

Governmental Factors

The nature of the Internet enables no one to control its structure and content, while as a recent phenomenon, laws and standards are yet to be developed and adopted to facilitate and regulate its commercial use. Some of the problems highlighted above are partly attributable to or greatly escalated by the lack of effective government involvement in promoting, facilitating and regulating e-commerce on the Internet.

Governments across the world have been slow in realising the potential of the Internet for economic growth and even slower in providing the necessary regulatory framework appropriate for conducting Net-based business. Although existing business laws and regulations are applicable to e-commerce, the particular nature of Internet-based business does requires special treatment, especially in the areas of security, fraud, sabotage, and data and consumer protection. Without the confidence and trust of those participating in the process, it will be impossible to achieve sustainable growth in e-commerce. However, censoring indecent and potentially criminal material on the Internet were often the main reasons chosen for regulation. In the UK, one of the advanced Net-economies, the Government put forward a draft Electronic Communications bill last year which deals with a wide range of issues central to the healthy development of e-commerce, including consumer protection, information security, authentication and digital signatures, confidentiality, encryption, taxation issues, intellectual property rights, technical standards, illegal content and so on.

As the Internet is a global computer network and e-commerce is essentially global business, the establishment of international standards and legal provisions for its smooth function is also critical. International bodies like the Organisation for Economic Cooperation and Development (OECD) and the European Union (EU) started to address some of the key issues in e-commerce from 1998, such as building trust in electronic commerce by ensuring the security and privacy of information and the protection of consumers; establishing ground rules for electronic transactions; and enhancing the information infrastructure through common interoperable standards, and access to open networks. However, progress is lamentably slow. It appears that each country will have to create their own Internet acceptable use policies, and figure out how to enforce them. Until then, the Internet will be a lawless frontier where anarchy and vigilantism are alive and well.

Legislation is of fundamental importance, but legal provisions only mark the boundary of unacceptable business practices and protect the consumer by redressing any illegal treatment. Consumers want to buy from companies that are not only law-abiding but more importantly are reliable and offer quality and value. Nevertheless, it is extremely difficult, if not impossible, to judge a company by its web site. Therefore, other measures must also be taken to boost consumer confidence in online shopping. The UK Government is trying to promote the ideas of 'e-hallmarks" which will guarantee that its users are legitimate traders offering assurances on security of payments and communications and giving accurate information on goods, prices and a returns policy. A new body -TrustUK - will be set up to accredit c-commerce codes and there are plans to market the c-hallmark internationally. However, many business organisations oppose the idea, wanting instead to rely on self-regulation without government intervention. For example, ABTA aims to clamp down on Internet sales by creating regulations for online travel transactions. It plans to publish a single revised code of conduct for agents and operators in May 2000, with a new section on Internet sales. It will require members to have a secure payment system if using the Internet to take bookings, and to observe the same ABTA rules as for other types of advertising.

The government can also play an active role in e-commerce by providing the necessary infrastructure for conducting Internet business. After all, the Internet was first started by Government - the US Department of Defence - in 1969 as ARPANet and only became commercialised in 1993. Uncertainty in many countries with regard to policies for investment, ownership, technology selection and general public access to the Internet has restricted the development of Net-based business and the penetration of Internet itself. Especially in the developing world, the huge investment required to establish the network and to make full use of it is out of reach of many businesses. In such circumstances, government could provide start-up funding for small companies. The UK government is also trying to close the gap between technology haves and have-nots and has launched an initiative to make computers available to low-income families for as little as £5 a month.

Wireless Services in Hospitality Companies

Wireless is allowing people and businesses to communicate and operate in ways that have historically been impossible. On its way to exploding into a multi-billion dollar industry in the next few years, wireless has already attracted millions of users. Hospitality companies have a unique opportunity to increase the value of their core products and services by providing a wireless infrastructure for customers to connect to the Internet, check e-mail and utilize corporate applications. In addition, there is a significant opportunity for businesses to benefit from the network by offering customized guest amenities and equipping employees with wireless devices to improve upon current operational inefficiencies.

As the first large retail chain to deploy wireless, Starbucks has established approximately 2,000 wireless-enabled stores worldwide. While there has been an abundance of positive publicity around the deployment, users accessing the network are few and far between. At each location, between one and five people are estimated to be using the service every month, at a rate of $6.00 per hour for one-time use or $39.99 per month for unlimited access. In a similar manner, McDonald's has recently begun a pilot deployment at 10 stores in New York city, with several hundred more planned by year end. Customers receive 60 minutes of wireless access free with the purchase of an Extra Value Meal or can buy access for $3. The deployments are too recent to confirm the degree of success, but the initial pattern seems to be similar to that of Starbucks with relatively low customer usage.

Wireless at McDonald's is a tougher sell because of the typical clientele. With more of a family-oriented environment than other merchants, McDonald's is generally not considered a place where typical customers would bring their laptops. With the model still in its infancy and almost certain to change, businesses must be creative to lure customers into using the infrastructure. One way to do this may include renovation of current facilities to cater to laptop-savvy customers by adding comfortable seats, wireless printers and a workspace with enough room for both a PC and a burger. Another option is to offer free telephone calls via voice-over IP (VOIP), a technology that sends voice over the network in a similar manner as data. While VOIP is currently in development, the functionality will offer significant opportunity for stores of the future.

Above and beyond providing customer access, wireless can offer customized customer experiences and improve upon current operational inefficiencies.In instances where speed of delivery makes or breaks a business, as is the case of McDonald's, creative 'line-buster' solutions can be deployed. These wireless tools range from remote ordering kiosks (staffed or unstaffed) and digital menu boards to devices that automatically control equipment.

Another area where wireless infrastructure is key is within the lodging space. Guest Internet access is becoming a standard amenity throughout the industry and travellers will soon find it as necessary as ice machines and cable television. Industry research recently conducted by IBM indicates the percentage of guests accessing wireless has been seen to exceed 20 percent in some cases, much greater than the uptake at food and beverage outlets. This is a key indicator that wireless is on the rise.

With a significant majority of hotels indicating Internet access can have an impact on occupancy, installing wireless needs to be considered in addition to wired solutions because of greater flexibility, faster implementation, fewer connectivity issues and reduced capital investment. In more and more cases, the availability of in-room, public space and meeting room access is a make-or-break decision for both the independent traveller and meeting planners of small and large group events.

Operational improvements can be realized when wireless devices are used for business functions such as check-in, check-out, bill printing, directions, concierge services, amenity requests, housekeeping, maintenance, point of sale, sales and catering and table management. While the number of these applications currently in use is minimal, redesigning today's core processes tied to wired solutions will allow hotels to operate more efficiently, empower the guests with more resources and respond to customer requests in a more prompt and accurate manner.

Wireless uses a family of specifications known as 802.11 to send high frequency signals to and from enabled devices. The most common standard today, 802.11b, provides acceptable connectivity speeds over a broad range of about 300 feet. Using a different approach, recently deployed 802.11a allows for faster data transmissions, but results in a relatively shorter range. In an attempt to improve upon both the connectivity speeds and range of 802.11a/b, 802.11g is currently in development.

Businesses implement wireless networks for customers and corporate applications two primary ways. In the first option, a local technology department installs access points as an extension of the wired solution. This allows the business to not only receive all revenue from the network but also tags it with the higher risk. The other option is to lease bandwidth from external providers such as telecom companies (T-Mobile, Sprint) or Cometa Networks, a joint venture of Intel, IBM and AT&T. In this revenue-sharing model, the provider ensures proper security, billing, bandwidth control, network maintenance and technical support.

Using a different approach than installing hotspots, the wireless Internet can also be found through a high-speed cellular system known as 2.5/3G. As an extension to the phone system, wireless devices are given an actual cellular phone number. While the technology is not widespread today and still under development, the portability and flexibility that is opened to users make it a technology that needs to be watched.

Security Issues

Gaps in current wireless standards (802.11a/b) expose some security concerns. The good news is that security is improving in parallel with this emerging technology. A wireless security standard known as 802.11i is targeted to be available the end of 2003. 802.11i is software that works on top of 802.11a/b to improve security features such as user authentication and key encryption. In addition, companies are utilizing other security techniques such as virtual private networks (VPN) to ensure that users access company information in a controlled environment. While the Internet will never be free from security issues, moving to the 802.11i standard in combination with other security measures at the device level allows wireless to be deployed throughout the industry without serious concerns.

Decision makers are not to be discouraged by today's low customer usage since wireless is still in its infancy. The introduction of wireless into daily life has focused to date on business travellers and will start to become mainstream in the next few years. The demand for communication anytime and anywhere is definitely on the rise. As an indicator of this explosion, Cometa Networks has pledged to roll out 20,000 hotspots in the United States by 2007. In addition, wireless is at the top of the list at Intel where the Centrino chipset, built specifically to run longer on battery power and connect more easily to wireless networks, was recently released.

With the tethers of wires removed, only a lack of creativity can limit the future possibilities of wireless. While the number of users today may not be impressive, the deployment of thousands of additional hotspots, decreased security concerns and more readily available wireless devices will strengthen today's demand and make it a commodity across all food and beverage facilities, coffee shops and hotels. Wireless must be considered today – and even more opportunity exists for the future. The potential value can serve as a competitive advantage by enhancing customer amenities and transforming fundamental business processes to bring about greater customer satisfaction and employee efficiency.

New Dimensions

Supported by the Internet the hospitality industry gets a new dimension of creating, supporting, presenting, conducting and selling its programs. Moreover, the hospitality industry is forced to leave the local principles of business performance, and to accept: new regulations as mentioned in the policy: "flunk ill local between the limits of a global positioning."

When trying to determine the hospitality industry activities supported by the Internet, it is necessary to differentiate between the two levels of service providing:

1) Providing more types of tourism services, including almost all aspects of tourism. This means that one tourism service provider can offer, for example: transportation, aceomodation, catering service, leisure facilities etc.

2) Providing only one aspect of a selective tourism service (a tourism service provider is in position, for example, to offer excllusivelly one specialized segment). This type of enterpreneur must be aware of customer targeting as a key to successful satisfaction of consumer demand, which is the fundamental determinant of all forms of businesses.

The two types of the hospitality industry activities supported by thr Internet have the following goals in common:

— to allow everyone to access the network,

— to make the local destination as competitive as possible (the reason for this is the expectation and convenience of customers to see all the options in one place),

— to establish themselves as competive within the local destination,

— to enable active cooperation with other suppliers offering other services (in this way all other customers needs can be met on one WEB site, e. g. in one place),

— to create checkable WEB sites applying criteria of infonnation quality checklist, which takes into consideration:

a) scope,

b) audience,

c) author,

d) authority or publishing body,

e) currency,

f) treatment,

g) arrangement /ease of use, and

h) regular up-dating,

— to provide same target customers with a service, regarding the tact that the customers significantly differ from each other according to the region of origin, nationality, religion, habits, customs, expectations and other socio-demographic characteristics,

— to adapt tourism offer to the new type of tourist, which might be referred to as Internet tourist 6. In order to get the profile of the majority of Internet tourists, Inemet market research should be used

Therefore, if not having a possiblity to meet a tourist's demand directly, a WEB site of a single tourism service provider should offer solutions of checked cooperators within the selected destination.

However, what might be considered a problem in the context of global service providing, is the fact that most of the travel products on sale over the Net are stored at various web sites owned and operated by individual companies, and in this way aggrevating selecting of all services a customer expects in the destination. Another problem is that the web does not always offer the lowest prices compared with the traditional distribution outlets's, what may discourage potential customers from booking directly on the web. All the facts mentioned above mean leaving the traditional concept of sharp competition in one destination, and approaching a concept of strong professional cooperation.

4

Hospitality Business in the New Economy

As hospitality industry executives contemplate the launch of the new millennium, they need to recognize the huge changes that are occurring in the way business is being conducted and begin planning in earnest as to how they will respond. For those operating within the physical world, the concept of electronic business or "e-business" may appear to be of limited significance. But such an assumption could be costly. E-business and its applications are undoubtedly the No. 1 topic in the boardrooms of most of the world's largest companies. The financial markets are making massive investments in the companies that deliver Internet technologies, content and related products and services, and the corporate world is now moving toward e-business offerings at a rapid clip.

On the business-to-business (b-to-b) front, e-business is projected to grow enormously in the United States over the next several years, with business-to-consumer (b-to-c) trade not as big, but growing just as fast. The McKenna Group estimates that the b-to-b marketplace could grow in value to US$500 billion in 2003. But those estimates may be low. General Motors Corporation, Ford Motor

Company and Daimler Chrysler, for example, have just announced that they plan to combine their efforts to form a b-to-b integrated supplier exchange through a single global portal. Meanwhile, on the retail front, the race is on to win the Internet consumer, whose ranks are growing rapidly. Traditional retailers have much to be concerned about as retail sales over the Internet skyrocket. And while such activity has yet to grow to the same extent in Europe and Asia/Pacific where the cost of phone calls remains an issue, it surely will over time. In the meantime, travel is one of the more popular online products for sale and over the next several years, it is projected in the United States alone to grow to US$12 billion.

E-business is rewriting the economic rules globally for every industry—including hospitality, travel and leisure. Indeed, it's important to recognize that we are now operating in what has been described as the "new economy," as global trends drive change, including globalization, consolidation, convergence, technology and communications. Even more, it is clear that the underlying sources of value are also changing. Use of intangible assets such as information, brands, customers, relationships and networks distinguish the most successful companies in the world.

It is clear that the Internet is having a huge impact on how we conduct our lives and our businesses. And it arrived virtually overnight. In the United States, for example, it took 38 years for television to get into 50 million homes. For the Internet, it took just five years. And for those U.S. consumers that are online, four out of five believe that the Internet is a more important invention than television. Of these same online consumers, close to six in 10 prefer e-mail to paper mail for business correspondence and over one in four check their e-mail while on vacation.

The Internet is also changing the customer relationship—undermining and redirecting customer attention to new sellers of products and services and away from their traditional relationships. And as this occurs, the traditional approaches that hospitality businesses have taken to distribution are all being affected.

From reservations taken over the Internet, which are projected to more than double to 9% of volume over the next year, to the declining role of the travel agent. This occurs as so-called "infomediaries" provide information and access, and software robots troll the activity online to develop matches between buyers and sellers, analyzing complex patterns and looking for trends for marketers to capitalize upon. As for the infomediaries, we can expect some of these to move into the transactions business and continue the process of disintermediation. For some hospitality companies, it may be best to join this new competition, particularly if it cannot be beaten at its own game.

The reality today is that the balance of power is shifting from sellers to buyers and in so doing it makes the importance of delivering high-quality service, convenience and value for money ever more compelling. The Internet has clearly leveled the playing field by making price information broadly available to the consumer. Internet business models affect product and services offerings, pricing, distribution and customer service, as well as long-term information capabilities. As a consequence, some hospitality suppliers will inevitably feed different tranches of their inventory through the various channels at their disposal—including the Internet, travel management organizations, destination packagers and the like.

In the end, customers want both convenience and consistency. They don't have all the leisure time that futurists once predicted they would have by now. In fact, they have less. Today's fast-paced world produces ever more stress, and consumers want information and they want it fast. And if hospitality companies and travel providers don't deliver convenience, somebody else inevitably will. They also want to be wired up to the rest of the world—at home, in their office and especially when they travel. And for hoteliers trying to cope with in-room technologies and the delivery of high-speed Internet access, we will soon be seeing more integration of network communication and entertainment products to further complicate or liberate our lives, depending on your point of view.

Customers are also looking for consistency—a simple concept, but central to whether a brand has value or not. And in the emerging networked world, aligning the value propositions of alliance partners and ensuring a seamless and consistent experience will only be as good as the weakest link in the chain.

Redefining the Value Chain for Consumers

Market wisdom today suggests that hospitality companies must embrace technology to compete against traditional competitors, as well as entrants that build their businesses with the latest technology and therefore bear the seal of a new economy entity. In this feverish environment of change, new models of distribution must be designed to lead the charge. More than any other aspect of business, the Internet revolution is reshaping the concept of the value chain, and how goods and services are distributed to consumers. To grow and succeed, management at hospitality and travel companies of any size must juggle multiple distribution channels, customer segments and intermediaries in their distribution of goods and services. All entities have zeroed in on a business-to-consumer strategy with the intent to influence purchase decisions and own consumer loyalty.

Classic economic models place the producer of goods at one end of the chain and the consumer on the other end, with packaging, shipping, storing and retail middlemen often connecting the two. The Internet, however, has redefined the traditional model and all of the relationships within this value chain. Regardless of whether the good is a product, a service or a combination of the two, the entire consumer purchasing process is undergoing re-evaluation with new business models poised to change or destroy the traditional methods of distribution. Although the hospitality industry began to adopt electronic commerce some 30 years ago when the airline industry developed automated reservation systems, technology is causing massive redesign of product distribution and value creation.

The logical consequence of eDistribution is inescapable: the traditional value chain collapses in what can be described as a "frictionless environment," as suppliers interact directly with consumers through networked technologies. In a frictionless environment, when interaction costs at the margin are close to zero, the cost structure and strategic implications of distribution clearly change very significantly.

In the so-called "old economy," distribution intermediaries existed to compensate for the lack of knowledge on products and pricing, as well as bringing buyer and seller together over a physical distance. As the Internet becomes the ultimate connectivity tool, however, products and services no longer require a physical distribution presence. Intermediaries can continue to contribute to the product or service. But as technology forces out physical inefficiencies in distribution, there are fewer places where middlemen can find safe haven from disintermediation.

The implications of a collapse of the traditional value chain are immense. Because much of the hospitality travel product is experienced-based, the role of distribution can be seen at its simplest as the ability to initiate an experience. Distribution, therefore, becomes part of the product itself. A redefined value chain has both positive and negative implications for each player in the chain. Generally speaking, suppliers benefit from lower distribution costs, better product image control, enhanced brand value and a better relationship with the customer. Intermediaries are likely to experience the greatest short-term turbulence, as each scrambles to assess the value they create and how to sustain it in the value chain. The consumer is most likely to gain, given the opportunity for better service, lower prices, tailored marketing and more options.

Traditional Suppliers

Regardless of distribution method, the products themselves, such as physical guest rooms, airline seats and rental cars, remain largely unchanged in the new economy, although customer information can be used to customize products and services. What is markedly different, however, is an extraordinary increase in competitive pressure to "own" the customer. Since connectivity to the customer is no longer a technology hurdle, each player in the value chain is attempting to develop customer loyalty. Owning or, at a minimum, significantly influencing the channel is an important component of managing customer loyalty.

Numerous supplier limitations have allowed nimble start-ups to take an early lead in the race to influence the consumer purchase decision. Who would have suspected that initially Expedia.com would sell more inventory than the Web sites of some of its suppliers? Most legacy information technology (IT) systems have not been engineered to handle the volume, content and query capabilities required of an online presence in the distribution channel. Customer relationship management (CRM) systems, for example, remain largely in an infancy stage - only the top few percent of frequent hotel guests for example, receive consistent customized service.

Indeed, the vast majority of Web site screens do not mimic how consumers buy hospitality and travel products and services. To secure a hotel booking online, for example, the customer typically enters an arrival date and length of stay. In reality these variables often are influenced by price, but this symbiotic relationship is not well represented at Web sites. Web sites will clearly need to provide more information and suggestions for customized and packaged travel if they are truly to serve the interests of travelers.

Consider the major issues for each of the key suppliers:

Airlines

The airlines have continued to be leaders in a shortening value chain by eliminating activities that do not add value, while developing such items as electronic ticketing and last-minute fares at low prices. Recently, five major airlines have announced they plan to create a megasite for eDistribution, a plan that responds to the threat of online travel agencies as they attempt to reintermediate themselves with customers. Whereas the airlines previously did not distribute their products directly to consumers, the new economy is requiring them to collaborate with their historical competitors with strategies to own the customer.

Hotel Companies

Channel conflict continues to be a significant issue among hotel companies. The price of a physical hotel room often varies widely depending on the source of booking (e.g., call center, Internet travel site, retail travel agency, corporate agent or direct contact with the property). Even though "single-image" inventory is widely favored in the industry, displaying the same image to all potential buyers remains challenging and is largely unfulfilled. Legacy reservation systems were not designed for true single image inventory. With available technology moving the industry toward price transparency, companies will feel intense pressure to compete on brand and differentiation, rather than price alone. Hotels must also manage additional customer touch points, an activity that is not always successful in the physical world. Guest recognition and tailored service are hallmarks of excellent properties. Customer relationship management is powered by good data, however, which remains a rarity within the hotel community. Extending recognition and consistency of service to the Internet and new sales channels compounds the problem of effectively managing the entire guest experience.

Traditional intermediaries

Changes brought by eDistribution have had the most profound effect on players that are positioned between suppliers and consumers in the distribution chain. These intermediaries are going through a period of transformation in how they do business:

Travel Agents: The retail travel agent is the best-known intermediary in the hospitality industry. A portion of a retailer's activities today remains value-added, while other roles are "old economy" in nature and becoming obsolete. The act of printing and issuing paper airline tickets is rooted in history when only Global Distribution System (GDS) terminals provided inventory access, and airlines required paper tickets for accounting. An area where travel agents do continue to add tremendous value is in advising travelers of destinations, tailoring travel to individual preferences, and saving time and money for the traveler before and during the trip. The new role for this group is that of knowledge manager.

Tour Operators: These intermediaries are also at significant risk from the collapse of the hospitality and travel value chain, as the Internet introduces new forms of competition. Tour operators aggregate travel products and repackage those products under a brand name. Tour operators in Europe own a much larger portion of the leisure travel market than in North America, with several large players dominating approximately half of the market. In the United States and Canada, the tour business is extremely fragmented, with few well-known brands and thin profit margins. Suppliers connected with consumer groups have the potential to mimic and exceed the purchasing power of individual tour operators. What prevents well-branded airline, hotel, and car rental companies from agreeing to share inventory and creating their own packages? Nothing - as is the case with many packages offered today by airlines and hotel companies. Furthermore, customer loyalty is often stronger with the travel agent that sells packages in North America.

Immense business and technology issues also exist for tour operators seeking to function in the new economy. Call centers create an artificial demand regulator, limiting the amount of product available on a free-sale basis by the number of agents answering calls. If the same model and IT systems are opened to Web traffic, a virtually unlimited amount of demand could overwhelm free-sale and price-yielding techniques that are designed for a different business model. To compete, tour operators will need to use networking tools and offer complete excursions that are priced in real-time and tailored to their customers.

GDS and Switches GDS providers offer some of the most reliably engineered IT transaction systems in existence. In a frictionless environment, however, Internet connectivity could ultimately eliminate the need for the GDS. GDS providers are now powering many of the virtual travel agent and online supplier bookings, and are demonstrating that intermediaries can still play an effective role by delivering reservation capabilities faster and cheaper than individual suppliers on their own.

The fact that the GDS and switching organizations such as THISCO and Wizcom are still used to book online travel indicates that new entrants have eliminated only a part of the traditional hospitality and travel value chain. Some friction in distribution still exists when these intermediaries are used to gain access to supplier inventory.

New dot.com intermediaries

Virtual travel agents represent a new form of intermediary, with some estimates placing the number of Web sites with travel booking capabilities at close to 1,000. Virtual travel agents charge a commission from suppliers (about 5 percent for hotels), but typically offer a lower flat fee for airlines. Many of these companies will clearly have to revisit their Internet strategies and business models over the next several years, as hotels, airlines and other suppliers become more aggressive in offering consumers direct access to inventory. Many of these new dot.com companies have yet to be profitable and are running out of time and money to gain significant market share to offset high costs in technology and payroll. New intermediaries such as Priceline.com have used the Internet to create a demand collection system. Worldres.com has amassed a central inventory of more than 11,000 properties, of which many are bed and breakfasts and vacation rentals that could not conform to the GDS listing requirements. A large number of additional entrants are expected in this arena in the next twelve months, particularly in the business-to-business arena, allowing corporations of all sizes to more effectively buy travel products.

Consumers

With the restructuring of the value chain, consumers stand to gain the most. Whether consumers choose to book online, or use the Internet for research and a physical travel agent to book, the level of knowledge, choices and convenience is unprecedented. The purchase experience will only improve as broadband access and multimedia content are married with product availability and one-to-one marketing activities. Distribution costs are eliminated when a value chain is shortened, and many of these savings are passed on to consumers in the form of bonus miles, last-minute fares and Web-direct-only pricing.

Vast amounts of information and the intensity of advertising "noise" can clearly be overwhelming to many consumers. But as the ease of use and customized offerings improve under the banner of powerful brands, the superiority of eBusiness applications for the hospitality and leisure industry will eventually become the norm. At that point, the new economy will no longer be "new," and the value chain will reflect the power of the Internet and its global networking capabilities.

Revenue Management Strategy

A revenue management strategy that incorporates all of the revenue drivers such as GDS, the web site and the electronic distribution channels is key. However, it requires the involvement of the sales department and all other profit centers of the hotel. This is unlike a budget in that a revenue strategy is renewable and adjustable where a budget is usually written in stone.

A sound revenue management strategy includes the optimum revenue mix and the tactics to achieve it — this is where the marketing plan comes in! "Managing" revenue is just that — it assumes an element of control in the revenue that you accept from various sources based upon cost of reservation, commissions, etc.

A revenue management strategy establishes "target" numbers to be achieved through a variety of ways; sales, manipulating the GDS, controlling the allocation and rate in the electronic distribution channels, etc. In other words, it is a pro-active rather than reactive function that simply turns the faucets on and off.

The sales strategies in the marketing plan flow from the revenue management strategy although sales is critical in developing it. The sales department is critical in that they have their fingers on the pulse of the market. They are responsible for assembling the economic information on market conditions and analyzing the potential threats to the market as well as identifying the opportunities. The sales department knows the potential of each market segment and the rate that each one will bear.

The development of the revenue management strategy allows sales to gage how many rooms in a given period they can book by market segment and at what rate. It also insures that existing and future group blocks won't be sabotaged by lower rates on the web site or distribution channels.

How exactly should this process work?

— *Gathering the info*: Each member of the team, but especially sales, should have been keeping information in regard to the market such as trends indicated by the

STR reports and other industry sources. Sales should take the temperature of top accounts to see what their forecasts for travel next year look like. The group logs pace reports for this year and next year should also be put into the file. Sales should also have the situation analysis completed as well as identified challenges and opportunities for the upcoming year.

— *Analyzing the Revenue Data:* The revenue reports should be analyzed to indicate the percentages currently generated by all revenue drivers. This, of course assumes that the data is accurate. If anyone has any doubts about the importance of proper market segment coding by reservations and the front desk they should end here. It is "GIGO" (garbage in — garbage out)! If there aren't accurate numbers, you will be playing a SWAG game.

— *The Facilitation*: This is the meeting of the minds, GM, sales, reservations and any other interested party such as the owner. They take a look at the budget, market conditions, all sources of revenue, etc. and begin projecting the revenue strategy by segment. This can be a contentious process as the sales department fights for accounts and room allocations by rate. However, as an associate once said, harmony is vastly overrated. This process can take several days as all of the evidence is presented and numbers are plugged into the model and adjusted — yada, yada. It never hurts to have an outside consultant facilitate this process to provide objective third party input.

— *The Final Product*: The spreadsheet, created from compromise that fulfills the requirement of the budget, becomes the basis of the revenue strategy. Every revenue driver is identified and the ideal mix of revenue and rate is there to yield the targeted REVPAR. Every revenue driver in the revenue strategy should have its own strategy and tactics section in the marketing plan — including the web site, the GDS strategy and the electronic distribution channels.

— *The Review Process*: The same fractious group that designed the strategy should meet periodically, it could be monthly or quarterly, to make adjustments based upon reality. In the initial development, "triggers" should have been identified that would automatically call for adjustments. Those triggers include unanticipated market changes, good or bad, changes in the economy and any national security breaches.

Account For Trade-Outs

There is a common arrangement in the hotel business where the hotel receives goods and/or services in exchange for rooms, food, and/or beverages. Overwhelmingly, trade-out is used to purchase advertising. This this arrangement is discueesd in this section.

Keep in mind the following points when doing trade-outs:

— The hotel is still the buyer and the advertising source is still the vendor. The only difference is the method of payment for the advertising. Instead of money, you are paying with goods and services.

— The contract should include the provision that the vendor is not to receive any portion of the rooms, food, or beverage until that amount of advertising has already been received. This is not barter; the hotel has purchased advertising and should not pay for anything it has not received.

— There should be an expiration date for the validity of the trade out (usually six to nine months). Clearly, the shorter, the better.

— The contract should exclude certain dates from availability, both for rooms, food, and beverage. Clearly, blackout all possible or close to sellout dates for rooms, among others. Also, exclude high traffic holidays from food and beverage such as Mothers Day, Valentine's Day, etc.

— The contract should specify the exact dollar value for each room, food, and beverage which they will receive, each good and service itemized. In addition, it is important to consider not giving dollar for dollar exchanges.

Make Exchanges Equal

The Director of Sales, in conjunction with Accounting, should determine the actual cost of what the hotel is exchanging for the advertising as the required analysis into whether or not to execute this arrangement.

For instance, the cost of providing one room night with a rack rate of $100.00 is different than the cost of providing one dinner priced at $100.00. Faced with costs of 25% in the Rooms Department versus 85% in the Food Department, the actual cost of giving them away is dramatically different. This analysis should be done prior to the execution of the contract.

Always separate the proportion of rooms, food, and beverage being exchanged and allocate a cost to each.

It is best to look at the average of the prior three months' expenses in each department, bearing in mind the time of year in which the vendor will be consuming the services to adjust these costs appropriately.

After the contract has been executed, Accounting should be given a copy of the cost calculations attached to a copy of the contract.

Invoicing and Record-keeping

When accounting receives an "invoice" for the advertising which has run, it is essential not to enter this into Accounts Payable.

Some vendors issue an actual invoice for the retail price of the advertising and those invoices can accidentally get entered into Accounts Payable. Because we have received the advertising, we have incurred a liability, but not a cash liability. The vendor is now free to consume rooms, food, or beverage according to the terms of the contract.

However, this liability does not belong in Accounts Payable and it is essential to keep all trade-out balances in a separate account which can be monitored separately from other payables.

Accounting should retrieve the contract from the files and determine the cost of the advertising which has been received on the basis of the proportion of rooms, food, and beverage in the arrangement. Assign a dollar amount of actual cost for the invoice to be written down to. The amount of advertising received must be determined either from the vendor or from the contract in order to assign the hotel's cost.

The first entry at the left illustrates how to enter the invoice easily and correctly.

Accounting

When the vendor has consumed the rooms, food or beverage, the vendor should sign for the services on the folio or check and it should be treated as other receivables. However, during the night audit or reconciliation process, this revenue and the settlement need to be adjusted off.

The steps for this depend upon your accounting system; that applies to the final entry necessary to complete this transaction, as illustrated in the second entry in the gray box.

Of course, the final entry depends on exactly what was consumed by the vendor in order to determine the allocation to the departments.

The foregoing entry provides both for the Accounting Department to ensure proper allocation and accounting of this transaction and for the relevant department incurring the actual cost of the advertising to be relieved of the costs and their impact on the departmental profit and percentages. If the departments are not receiving any revenue from these guests or patrons, they should be credited with the associated costs. This transaction is to reduce advertising expense and Sales & Marketing should incur the total cost of this transaction.

A final and very important point: consult with your Certified Public Accountant, lawyer or other competent professional before implementing any procedure like this. Tax laws change frequently and taxes, particularly sales taxes, may be impacted. Neither the author nor this publication assume any responsibility for the consequences of using these procedures and do not intend to set policies and/or procedures for individual properties or the hotel industry.

Banks and Credit Companies as Hotel Owners

One of the most unwilling and therefore unhappy hotel owners is a bank or credit company which has a hotel in its real estate owned (REO) portfolio, while it tries to work its way out of the problem loan.

Lenders in this situation have two primary goals. The lender's first goal is to stop loosing money. The easiest way to accomplish this goal is to quit putting money into the hotel. Their second goal is to put the hotel on the market and sell it as quickly as possible. These are not unreasonable goals. Whoever the lender may hire to act on its behalf as management will only keep its assignment and get additional assignments if these goals are understood.

The issue of putting additional money into the hotel may be a moot point if the business was not covering capital costs but was generating sufficient cash to pay real estate taxes and insurance . If there is insufficient business volume to cover normal operating expenses several issues need to be addressed. One is to reduce expenses from normal to painfully low without having a negative impact on income. Any idea which will produce additional income must be considered. Finally, the lender (owner in this case) must be asked for additional funds by means of a cash flow forecast and business plan. This effort assumes that the lender realizes a hotel sells quicker and for a higher price when it is operating as opposed to closed.

Reducing expenses to minimal levels takes a great deal of care. All business owners aspire to this goal, however, none intentionally try to go to the very edge and most try to keep a long term outlook.

For a lender there is no long term, only the time from when the hotel was acquired until it is sold. A hotel will sell more quickly and for a higher price if its physical appearance is good and sales are showing an upward trend. A sophisticated lender will work with management to find a balance regarding expenses.

It takes money to make money is a cliche which has merit. Coming up with ideas to increase sales in a hotel is not difficult. The difficulty lies in singling out a number of very cost effective ideas which the market will react to quickly. Lowering room rates usually does not work. Insuring fundamentals such as room cleanliness, employee training and attitudes, maintenance and the quality of guest supplies are competitive will go a long way towards maintaining the current customer base.

Once these things are done, consideration should be given to actually raising room rates and developing a more sophisticated pricing strategy. Making quality outside sales calls always results in improved sales. Nothing produces better results than going out, identifying potential sources of business, meeting their needs and subsequently asking for the business. Giving up a few dollars of income to increase the price value perception is usually worthwhile because often these hotels already suffer from a poor image. Free local phone calls appeals to commercial guests. Free breakfast appeals to all and may contribute to lowering losses if the hotel has a restaurant which is loosing money while trying to serve a full breakfast menu.

Helping the lender and their real estate agents sell the property is a key function of independent management. The role of hotel management in this case is to insure that the hotel shows well and is an extension of the subjects previously discussed. Working with the hotel's employees during this period to help them understand the situation and its potential impact on them ,usually very little, is critical. Another area where management can help is in pricing the property for sale and in developing a marketing strategy. If competent management is retained they should have an understanding of hotel values under a variety of circumstances. Additionally, they should know how to explain the hotel's potential better than the lender or the Realtor and they may be the most credible sales representative available.

Working together, assuming there are no lengthy legal delays, the lender and the management company can get the hotel off the lenders REO portfolio in a reasonable amount of time.

Fixed Expenses

Somewhere on most hotel financial statements, usually towards the bottom, is a major heading called Fixed Expenses. General Managers and Comptrollers created this title for two reasons. Either owners handled the items bundled in there or General Manger and Comptrollers didn't want to assume responsibility for the items they placed there.

Fixed Expenses usually includes items such as rent, real estate taxes, personal property taxes, building and contents insurance, interest expense, depreciation and amortization.

Other items which might appear there are equipment leases, cable TV and who knows what else occasionally. While not classified as fixed expenses, payroll taxes, unemployment insurance and other benefits - both those discretionary to the operation and those which are mandated by government regulation - are thought of as fixed expenses by many hoteliers.

We don't believe there is a fixed expense in a hotel. There are simply some expenses which take longer to reduce than others! Many of these are the same ones that can be controlled by planning and negotiation when the acquisition or development is planned.

General Managers and Comptrollers (management) should not divorce themselves from these issues any more than an owner would. One way an owner can enhance these key employees' interest in these expenses is to make their incentive pay tied to his or her real profitability. This is also t rue of management company incentive fees.

Real Estate Taxes

Management can help the owner in a number of ways with these different expenses in addition to increasing revenues to cover them. An an example, real estate taxes are usually considered outside of the control of management.

Real estate tax assessments, their calculations and their payment are a matter of public record. By research other hotels' tax rates at the county offices and understanding their calculations, management can begin to ascertain whether the taxes assessed their particular hotel are relatively fair or not.

If they appear to be unfairly high relative to the competition and the hotel's circumstances, management can, at a minimum, sit down with the tax assessor and discuss the issue. S/he will answer questions, ask for more information and possibly lower the taxes. In areas where there are personal property taxes, the system works much the same way.

If the taxes are apparently unfairly high and the assessor does not agree, management, with the owner's approval, can begin the appeals process. In a simple case, much of the work can be done by management. There are lawyers who specialize in this area of the law. They can be retained on a fee or contingency basis. Real estate taxes should be examined every three or four years, depending upon local circumstances.

Workers Compensation

Workers compensation insurance can be attacked from several directions. The most obvious is to in sure that all employees are properly classified because different classifications have difference insurance rates applied to them.

Next, management should insure that workers compensation insurance is being bought from the least expensive source available to a particular hotel.

Another factor affecting workers compensation insurance is a particular location's injury experience. Records of previous losses must be reviewed and action taken, either through staff training, physical changes in the hotel or in methods of accomplishing tasks.

Remember, even an injury sustained while walking out to their car can result in an accepted workers compensation claim. We had one workers compensation claim for an employee who tripped over a cat on the way to her car.

In Minnesota, the law and regulations promulgated based on that law have created a burdensome system. The limits are high, the definition of injuries, the time limits and the bureaucracy all contribute to one of the highest expenses in the Midwest. By lobbying together and making legislatures and the administration aware of the problem, management can contribute to reducing this expense.

Minimum Wage

Minimum wage is also a "fixed expense" by acting as a baseline for wages. At the state and national levels, one must participate in the process of government to affect change. Other than managing your labor force more efficiently, reducing staff and lowering service to your guests, the only control management has over this expense is through joining with others in the hospitality industry through the state and national hospitality associations.

Interest and Lease Expenses

Getting your interest and lease expenses reduced may be as difficult as reducing government-mandated expenses. Interest and lease expenses are negotiable at the time the agreements are entered into. Many times they can be reduced simply by asking at a later time.

The hammer management has is the lender/lessor knowing that you can go out and g get a new loan, buy out the lease or do business in the future with another lender or leasing company.

It is a difficult and time consuming task, but a worthwhile one. Given the recent increase in interest rates, deals made in the most recent few years may be as good as they can be for the foreseeable future.-Work with your owner and network with your local banks. You should at least be able to g get their rooms, meeting and party business!

When considering new loans or leases, remember that the items or equipment you are purchasing are a separate transaction from the loan or lease. Just like soap and toilet paper are commodities, so is money. No lender or leasing company is doing you a favor by giving you access to money. You are a customer helping them reach a sales budget. Shop for the best deal. The leasing company suggested by the vendor m may not necessarily offer the best deal.

Insurance Cost

Insurance of all types is a completely controllable expense within certain limits. Deductibles, co-payments and proper valuation of the building and furniture, fixtures and equipment replacement cost are all components of the insurance premium. The hotel's loss record enters into the calculation also. Changes in any or all of these items will affect your premium cost.

Different insurance companies charge different rates for insuring hotels based on their loss experience and appetite for hotel insurance risk at a particular time.

Work with your in insurance agent to understand what and where s/he has been shopping for your insurance. Are the companies (agencies refer to insurance companies as "markets") your agency has been considering regular insurers of hotels? Ask your agent why s/he doesn't investigate other markets. Use two agencies and have the second agency shop other markets. Look for agencies which have several other hotel clients and experience handling hotel claims. If you have the financial stature to do so, give serious consideration to self-insurance.

Cable and satellite TV expense are also manageable. Reducing premium channels offerings is a quick way to reduce cable expense. Don't let cable companies fool you with their claims of regulations and community controlled tariffs. Usually those only apply to residential consumers.

Look into pay-per-view providers such as SpectraVision and satellite companies now so you will be prepared when the current cable contract expires. In many cases, pay-per-view can be layered on top of the cable system so the hotel can earn some offsetting revenues.

In summary, look at fixed expenses just as you would any other expense. You can often make a greater impact on the bottomline through these items than by reducing food cost and they are not as difficult to maintain.

Cost of Capital and its Impact

Capital for hotel ventures typically consists of two components, debt and equity. Their costs are the interest on the debt, the investors' expected return on equity and the cost of obtaining the capital itself. Some of the cost of raising capital can initially be folded back into the debt or equity but in the end it is paid for with additional interest or less profit distribution.

The cost of debt actually includes several different components. Among the possible components are mortgage origination fees, mortgage brokerage commissions, points, prepayment penalties (if one prepays later in order to obtain better terms from another source), legal fees (the borrower's and the lender's), appraisal fee, environmental study fee, and finally interest. The component with the most impact over time is interest.

Interest rates charged for commercial mortgages are impacted by a number of factors. These might include, but are not limited to, the term of the loan, whether the interest rate is variable or fixed, the basis on which the variable interest moves and the amount it can fluctuate in any one period, interest rates at the time the loan commitment is made, the actual source of the funds the lender will be using to make the mortgage loan and a lot of issues that are purely subjective..

These subjective items include the lender's perception of these items: the risk of the hotel project relative to the other loans that could be made; the ultimate value of the collateral; the financial stability of the borrowing entity and its principals; quality of management; and if the project "fits" in the lender's loan portfolio relative to the type of project it is. Where the lender stands relative to achieving their lending goals for the time period and the political strength of the particular person carrying the loan through the underwriting process are also major factors. Aside from looking at debt coverage ratios and loan to value ratios the lender is going to consider all these other factors at some level. They will all ultimately affect the amount of the loan and the terms. Every aspect of the terms has a relative cost to the borrower.

For instance a lender may make the borrower escrow funds to complete certain required improvements in the hotel. Distribution of those funds will not be done until they receive all documentation that the improvements are completed, paid for and lien releases obtained. This means the borrower has to come up with the funds from other sources until the lender releases the funds. There is a cost to those additional funds, either additional interest or opportunity cost because they are not invested elsewhere.

If the escrow agreement is written so that the bank will pay for the improvements from the escrow fund as they are completed the borrower may not have to come up with as much extra money. The lender, however, is now assuming some risk that the projects will, in fact, be completed. For this to work efficiently for the lender, borrower and contractors, the escrow agreements and contracts for construction all have to be coordinated to all parties' satisfaction.

The cost of coordinating these items will show up as time, legal fees and probably higher prices from the contractor. The point here is that a hotel developer with sufficient capital does not have to do these things or bear these costs. This savings increases the return on the investment as compared to a developer with less capital.

If the lender perceives one borrower and his or her project to be less risky than another's they may grant more favorable terms in the loan in the form of slightly lower interest. On the surface the impact of this may not be significant but the reality is quite different. For instance on a $10,000,000 project with a $7,500,000 mortgage for 20 years the difference between an interest rate of 8.5% and 8.25% is $14,184 in principal and interest payments. If one disregards the tax implications of this and only evaluates the cash on cash return on equity the difference is just over a half a percentage point.

If the investors were going to receive an average cash on cash return on equity from operations of 19.65% with the 8.5% percent interest rate they will now receive one of 20.217%. Which developer will have the easier time raising equity capital? Among other things easier means less costly. And less costly also translates into even higher returns on equity.

While one doesn't usually think of equity as having a cost it does. In the simplest terms an individual investor has choices as to where s/he might invest. These alternatives all have different levels of expected return and risk. The higher the perceived risk the higher the expected return. If this investor could have invested in a government backed security and had a return of 6.0% without risk then their perceived cost is at least that amount. If they are going to take the risk of investing in something they know nothing about, have no control over and which has no liquidity they are going to have a much higher expectation for their investment return. The developer is probably going to have to forego some return until the investors' expectations are met. This is a cost of capital to the developer.

Another example might be when the developer is larger and decides to go to the public for the equity.

Whether the approach is through a registered private placement memorandum or a small stock offering there will be significant legal, accounting and other fees associated with the fund raising project. Depending on the planned source of funds, the size of the fund raising has to be greater than a certain amount to justify these methods.

On the other hand a major publicly traded REIT (Real Estate Investment Trust) or C corporation has already gone to this expense. So much money, hundreds of millions or more, has been raised that the cost of the funds is relatively low relative to interest rates. Such a company will simply buy a hotel for cash from their cash reserves or credit lines in a very short process and if appropriate get a mortgage at their leisure on very favorable terms.

Because they were able to act quickly and pay all cash to the seller this buyer probably obtained much more favorable terms on the purchase. As a further point, because their cost of capital was so much lower their earnings expectations do not need to be as high as the smaller entity with the higher cost of capital. It is this relationship to the cost of capital that makes these companies appear to overpay for existing hotels as viewed from the smaller entities' perspective.

By driving up the price of existing hotels, these companies lower the achievable returns of the smaller companies when both are seeking the same types of hotels. This is one reason smaller companies seek out hotels to buy that the larger companies may not pursue for one reason or another.

The smaller company needs to deal with sellers who are patient and wait while the capital for the purchase is raised. The seller will wait because they have been unable to sell it to another buyer or because the price is higher. In either case the return will be lower or the risk is higher for the buyer. After all, why wouldn't anyone else buy the hotel? In the end, the company with less capital cannot afford to make mistakes and has to maximize cash flow by being a very good hotel marketer and operator. The company with more capital and higher returns can, of course, afford to pay premium wages to its key executives and other staff. The cost and availability of capital affects every aspect of competition in the hotel industry in very fundamental ways.

Advantages of Urban Timeshare in Hospitality Industry

Urban timeshare has inspired intense interest during the past two years with forecasts that it will be a new wave of product in a growing industry. Yet the record speaks to a slow start for this sector. The timeshare industry at large has continued to thrive with growth posted at 16 percent annually in sales volume since 1980. Operators have found the industry resilient to both economic and lodging downturns. High returns and growth opportunities are forecast for both hotels and independent operators with the industry's credibility and opportunities on the rise as reputable developers join the sector. The latest high-profile entrant promises to aid consumers in evaluating alternative products. Thomas Cook, the giant travel company, has announced it will represent high-quality timeshare properties. The entry of this well known name offers a significant boost for all reputable timeshare businesses.

Even with the strength of the timeshare industry generally, development of urban timeshare projects has lagged To date, just three urban developments are creating a standard The Manhattan Club in New York, Marriott's Custom House resort in Boston; and The Edinburgh Residence in Scotland. Urban timeshare would appear to offer distinct advantages to the hospitality industry, but it has yet to be developed to any great degree by companies. A combination of market forces and industry challenges have created short-term hurdles. The long-term prognosis, however, may offer opportunities for developers in a niche sector attracting sophisticated, upscale buyers, who are interested in the urban experience.

One of the major advantages timeshare products offer hospitality groups is the resilience of the sector to economic downturn. With the exception of a small decline in sales volumes in 1985, American Resort Development Association (ARDA) statistics suggest that timeshare sales have survived the peaks and troughs characterising the hospitality industry Timeshare occupancy tends to be more predictable, and the manager of the timeshare units finds it far easier to manage variable costs, particularly labour, than his or her counterpart in the hotel business. Despite the undisputed interest of almost all major hospitality groups, however r, only Marriott has made a large-scale commitment to the concept outside the United States.

The initial economics of urban timeshare look beguiling to a developer. The average cost of development of a five-star London hotel room can be anything up to £225,000 per room (when an existing property is converted). For a 300-room hotel, this brings the development price to £67.5 million. After adding 10 percent uplift for additional facilities to be offered, the total product cost would amount to approximately £74.25

million. Consider the economic return if that same project were developed as a timeshare. Assuming a sales price of approximately £17,500 per week, and 50 weeks of occupancy per year, total income would amount to £262.5 million. On this basis, sales of just 15 weeks of inventory would fully cover the product cost. Assuming administrative/overhead costs of 10% (i.e., approximately £26 million), our hypothetical urban timeshare would yield a staggering £162 million (62 percent of the total cost) to cover sales and marketing expenses, and profits.

The "numbers" are clearly tantalizing. Two key reasons, however, have mitigated against urban timeshare;

— the increased profile and attractiveness of timeshare has coincided with a property boom in the major cities; and

— inability to control marketing costs.

In the London market, for example, many developers and botchers alike have considered the viability of timeshare, either on a stand - alone basis or as a mixed-use plan. Property prices have escalated over the past few years, however. At the same time, the return that can be generated from other options (such as serviced apartments) has been sufficiently high to discourage companies from developing an urban timeshare, particularly with the additional risk associated principally with the marketing costs.

Resort timeshares have been successful, in part due to differential pricing and high occupancy rates achieved throughout the year as a result of an attractive climate and a variety of recreational amenities. Likewise, urban timeshare must also be based in locations that can attract visitors throughout the year. In the case of city sites, customers also include corporations. which may buy blocks of weeks. For these reasons, areas just outside New York, London and Paris have been regarded as the most attractive locations.

The New York Manhattan Club is perhaps the best example of this type of development. Developed by the Eichner family, which builds and owns retail, commercial and residential properties, The Manhattan Club offers high specification suites with an average size of 650 square feet. The original sale price of $15,000 per week has climbed to $21,000. The site actually opened in August, 1997, and to date approximately 16 percent (i.e., 3,000 weeks) have been sold out of a total 18,000 weeks. The total site cost $60 million, of which half has been made available to timeshare, and the refurbishment of the timeshare element is estimated at $70 million. Approximate revenues to date based on 3,000 weeks sold at an average price of $15,000 amount to some $45 million, which provides very substantial cash flow to finance the continuing development. Multiple weeks have been sold to corporations for use by company employees. Surprisingly, sales to individuals are typically made to people living within a 90-minute radius of New York. Heavily used by owners, opportunities for exchanging into The Manhattan Club are fairly limited, although it is affiliated to the RCI exchange network.

The Edinburgh Residence in Edinburgh, Scotland, represents one of the best examples of urban timeshare outside the United States. Three directors, all of whom had previously worked in the timeshare business, set up the Edinburgh Residence project. These individuals recognized the gap in the market for flexible urban timeshares, which could exploit the "short break" market.

Edinburgh represents a fairly unusual location for European urban timeshares because it does not typically offer the corporate customer potential of cities such as New York, London or Boston. Occupancy is smoothed throughout the year using the RCI exchange, with approximately 10 percent of clients taking advantage of the exchange programme.

Financing Issues

Once a timeshare site is identified, financing becomes a major issue. particularly for companies that are not well established. There is still widespread institutional anxiety among finance providers for timeshare developments. Those developers able to obtain development finance generally have an existing relationship with the institution and a track record in timeshare / timeshare sales. In this regard, distribution capacity is regarded as key. The timeshare developer must have a sound business plan with a focus on, and substantiation of, the projected sales volumes. Extensive due diligence is carried out, usually both by the developer and the institution. Moreover, large projects ($50 million +) are preferred to smaller projects. Depending on the structure of the timeshare development, there may be additional security required.

In the United States, only a few institutions will participate in timeshare financing. There are three or four specialist lenders, of which the most notable is Finova. Those lenders specialising in financing will provide the construction loan principally to secure the provision of consumer financing. In the United kingdom and Europe, banks and credit institutions generally lend only to timeshare on the back of existing relationships. Many of the high street banking names are reluctant to provide loans to the industry, although specialist finance providers are beginning to appear. Finova now has a European presence, for example. Construction finance for the new players is still very difficult.

The Edinburgh Residence was an exception to this rule. One-third of the financing was provided by 3i (Glasgow) and Aberdeen Asset Managers (U.K. venture capitalists), while two-thirds came from the Royal Bank of Scotland. Agreeing the funding for the project is regarded as the biggest single achievement of the project directors and is largely attributed to finding the right people. The refurbishment of the Edinburgh Residence was done successfully, and confidence amongst the finance providers has accordingly grown. The first 10 suites of The Edinburgh Residence were opened on February 1, 1997. Royal Bank of Scotland then accelerated the funding so that all 30 of the suites were opened by late July, 1997.

Marketing and Sales

In many respects, marketing and sales costs are the "great unknown" as regards timeshare in general, but more particularly urban timeshare. where there is far less experience on which accurate predictions can he made. The average active project reports marketing and sales costs of 38.5 percent, although 48.2 percent of projects have marketing and sales costs of more than 40 percent. Moreover, the three major urban timeshares have unique profiles. The marketing programme of Marriott's Custom house in Boston is highly developed, for example, as one of a number of timeshare developments owned by the hotel company.

When a project is confined to a single site, the marketing of an urban timeshare development is a much more difficult problem. The key issue is balancing the need to generate leads and achieve a high conversion rate, whilst minimising marketing costs. The Manhattan Club, for example, sends targeted mailings through credit card companies, and advertises in publications such as theatre brochures and broadsheets. The timeshare achieves a 20-25 percent conversion rate with 400-500 families visiting the site a week. The Edinburgh Residence, on the other hand, uses a third-party company to do its marketing. Like The Manhattan Club, it relies on direct mail and displayed advertisements in the broadsheets. However, it also gains a substantial proportion of its customers through in-house affinity relationships in the form of promotional deals. Its total marketing costs amount to only 18 percent of the cost base, which is substantially lower than the industry as a whole. Conversion rates are approximately 30 percent, in contrast to the average market rare of approximately 15 percent.

Maintenance Fees

In the recent RCI consulting study on the resort timeshare industry in the United States, average maintenance fees ranged from $270 for a studio unit to $425 for a three bedroom unit with an overall weighted average of $360 per week. The maintenance fee for both The Manhattan Club and the Custom House development is $575 per week, or approximately $82 a night. This is clearly at the top end of the market. The Edinburgh Residence's annual maintenance fee, on the other hand, at £195 per week per annum is regarded as inexpensive by approximately 95 percent of the clients, according to management. At approximately £28 per day, this is certainly towards the lower end of expectations. As yet, maintenance fees in general do not seem to reflect the added advantage which timeshare providers should achieve from the ability to manage costs better. With the increased transparency in the market produced by initiatives such as the Thomas Cook entry, competition to keep down maintenance fees is expected to increase.

New Developments

The Thomas Cook entry into the timeshare market is undoubtedly the most significant development in timeshare in recent years. The company announced at the beginning of June that a number of its sales outlets would represent four-star and above-quality properties built by reputable developers. Thomas Cook retail outlets are expected to offer a range of timeshare, although the company's role is understood to be one of marketing rather than closing sales. The advantage to the consumer should be the increased transparency of products offered by developers. Previously, potential customers have had to do their own research. From a developer's point of view, there are a number of attractions. A customer entering the process through Thomas Cook may be more favourably predisposed toward the product. This may improve conversion ratios compared to the typical customer who has responded to a direct marketing initiative. For those high quality developers that have only one or two sites, it should help to alleviate the need for an expensive marketing team whilst benefiting from the economies of scale which Thomas Cook can achieve by marketing several different projects. In addition, Thomas Cook obviously has the ability to arrange flights and rental cars to transport people to the Site without the need to involve an additional party. Overall, this should help reduce the administrative costs incurred by the developer.

Urban timesharing may be slow to get off the ground, but it still offers great potential. Once property prices begin to soften in major cities, the industry can expect more entrants into urban timeshare. For high - quality developments in Europe, Thomas Cook should have a positive impact on individual ownership of both resort and urban timeshare. It is likely, however, that the urban timeshare purchaser will be a more sophisticated upscale buyer. The surprising trend seen in the up-market developments to date is the attraction they have held for people within a relatively short radius of the metropolitan centre. Once more up-market urban timeshare becomes available, this trend is likely to be less marked.

Notwithstanding the potential attractiveness of urban timeshare to individuals, the real breakthrough is likely to come as more corporations become buyers of timeshare weeks. This is likely to occur when the cost of acquiring and maintaining an urban timeshare compares more favourably with the cost of hotel rooms, when corporate discounts are taken into account. With increased transparency of costs and better yield management, which timeshare developers should be able to achieve, a gradual decline in the annual maintenance fee is anticipated. Once this occurs, and developers are able to provide satisfactory quality assurance, interest is likely to grow in the corporate market. As the resale market in such property develops, this should also enhance interest. particularly if the timeshare weeks hold their price.

5

Challenges of Hospitality Marketing

The current economic slowdown represents a major challenge for the hospitality industry. Many hotels and restaurants have weathered the storm by slashing budgets, laying off employees, and reducing guest amenities. Although these tactics have allowed the hospitality industry to stem its short-term losses, they are not long-term solutions.

In response to this challenge, more hotels and restaurants have turned to Internet-and network-enabled business solutions. In the United States, for example, a 2001 National Restaurant Association survey revealed that more than half of all restaurant operators now access the Internet for business-related purposes, including marketing, training, and communications. In the hotel industry, in-room amenities such as high-speed Internet access and video-on-demand have become must-have items for business travellers. Wireless networks also play an increasingly vital role, linking together everything from point-of-sale terminals to housekeeping and security management systems.

As a result of these innovations, the hospitality industry has discovered that it is possible to cut labour and overhead costs without sacrificing product quality or customer service. These solutions are relevant to hospitality-related businesses of every size, from single-unit operations to multinational corporations.

According to the US National Restaurant Association, the U.S. restaurant industry in 2001 suffered its slowest sales growth in a decade, and 2002 sales growth will remain below average. The hotel industry in the United States suffered an even more dramatic decline; average room occupancy rates in late 2001 dropped by as much as 30 to 40% before recovering somewhat during the first months of 2002.

According to Barry Goldstein, a strategist for the Cisco Systems Internet Business Solutions Group, recent improvements in the industry's fortunes come with a caveat: Among hotels in the United States, the recovery is happening at lower price points-an average of 25% lower. "Hotels must find a way to drive additional customer revenue while increasing employee productivity," Goldstein says.

Restaurants face a similar dilemma. In addition to building customer demand for high-margin menu items, restaurant operators must manage food and overhead costs more carefully than ever before. Achieving these goals, in turn, requires operators to track inventories, food use, payroll, and other key metrics as accurately as possible-an especially difficult task for geographically dispersed, multi-unit operations.

The hotel industry faces additional problems maintaining established revenue sources. Income from guest phone calls, for example, has declined substantially as more travelers use wireless phones. According to Goldstein, one major hotel chain expects a $90 million shortfall in phone-related revenue, reflecting a continuing long-term decline in a major source of income for large and small hotel operators alike. "The question is," Goldstein says, "how do you make up that difference with revenue from other sources?"

Hospitality businesses also face constraints on their ability to apply traditional network-enabled business solutions:

— Hotel and restaurant chains often include multiple business units, widely scattered across the United States and around the world.

— Expensive, time-consuming, and disruptive physical infrastructure upgrades are not an option for many hotels and restaurants.

— Hotel and restaurant employees are highly mobile, work irregular hours, and rarely have access to traditional offices and computers.

— Technological solutions must enhance opportunities to provide "high-touch," personalized customer service-not replace them.

Network-enabled Solutions

Restaurants and hotels can now choose from a variety of network-enabled solutions tailored to meet their business needs. These technologies emphasize speed and flexibility; work well with a distributed, mobile workforce; and leverage existing infrastructure and business methods. Examples of these technologies include:

— Wireless local-area networks

— Internet-based e-learning tools

— Web-based hosted applications

— Broadband Internet access

— Voice over Internet Protocol services

— Virtual private network technology

When applied to the hospitality industry, these technologies offer a variety of compelling business solutions:

— Wireless point-of-sale systems that keep restaurant servers on the floor, streamline the order-taking process, and minimize mistakes

— E-learning applications that allow hospitality employees to receive on-demand training, regardless of where or when they work

— A new generation of revenue-generating guest services, including broadband Internet access, video-on-demand, and Internet-enabled telephony systems

— Web-based profit-and-loss accounting, invoicing, payroll, and point-of-sale systems that link to enterprise systems at corporate headquarters and reduce technology overhead costs at individual business units

— Kitchen management systems that use the Internet to communicate with vendors and suppliers, automatically scheduling food orders, updating inventories, and even tracking food safety data

Benefits

Many of these solutions deliver quantifiable results; according to one study, wireless point-of-sale systems in a full-service restaurant can increase service speed 20 to 30% while dramatically decreasing waste-related food costs.

Other quantifiable benefits from employing Internet-based and network-enabled applications include:

— Lower labour costs and higher productivity—According to Joe Skorupa, editor of Hospitality Technology magazine, a wireless point-of-sale system in a full-service restaurant makes it possible for fewer servers to generate more per-customer revenue. "High-margin items like desserts and beverages require up-selling," Skorupa says, "and that requires the servers to spend more time interacting with customers."

— Reduced infrastructure upgrade costs—Cisco long-reach Ethernet technology allows hotels to provide broad-band Internet access and related services via existing phone lines-potentially saving thousands of dollars in cabling and other infrastructure upgrade expenses. Wireless networks extend connectivity to both guests and staff in areas where wiring isn't available, such as hotel lobbies or meeting rooms. Wireless networks at the front door enable mobile check-in services, improving both employee productivity and customer satisfaction.

— Streamlined business operations—The flow of information between business units and corporate headquarters can create a costly bottleneck for multi-unit hotels and restaurants. Web-based applications eliminate this problem, giving managers immediate, detailed access to any operating unit's profit-and-loss statements, payroll, inventory, and other vital data.

As Steve Nye, general manager of the Cisco Building Broadband Solutions unit, notes, these technologies provide other benefits that may be hard to quantify but are vital nevertheless. "Hotels see [Internet access] as part of their competitive advantage; it puts people in the rooms and boosts occupancy rates, creating other revenue opportunities," he says. Nye adds that many business travelers now view such amenities as a "check-off" item when they select a hotel; as a result, properties that can't offer such services wili lose business to those that do.

The benefits of Internet connectivity and related technologies are not limited to large, multi-unit hospitality operations. A single-unit full-service restaurant, for example, can benefit from a wireless point-of-sale solution that improves staff communication and cuts labour costs.

Importance of Advocacy in Hospitality Marketing

Most hospitality marketers recognize the importance of advocacy— word of mouth referrals—in fuelling demand for their travel and tourism products. Referrals are the highest-ranked source of information consumers use to select travel services, according to a 1998 report by the Travel Industry Association of America.

Even academic studies have confirmed the important role of word of mouth. However, the same studies also conclude that marketers must invest more heavily in magazines, television, newspapers and travel agencies; that they're not doing enough in those areas to maximize promotion of their operations and thus gain significantly more business.

A high percentage of sales come from word of mouth, yet according to these studies, travel marketers are not doing enough mass marketing? If referrals from satisfied customers represent the most successful avenue to attracting new clients, does it make sense for the marketers to send almost all their budgets in another direction, toward on mass marketing channels? This view is misguided when it encourages marketers to hurl hundreds upon thousands of dollars at conventional communications channels despite common knowledge and clear evidence that certain less conventional alternatives, i.e., word of mouth techniques, have been shown to be far more cost-effective and promise greater returns.

Could travel marketers then do a better job attracting new customers, and keeping "old" customers coming back, if more budgets were directed toward enhanced word-of-mouth programs? The research seems to conclude so, suggesting that a comparatively smaller investment in "customer advocacy" marketing can be expected to yield a higher return on investment dollars. Although it's certainly true that word of mouth can't do it all by itself, this avenue is typically vastly over-looked for its power to do what it can.

In today's marketing environment, in fact, travel firms attempting to reach target consumers through traditional brand-building approaches, such as advertising and customer-loyalty programs, face higher hurdles than ever before. Advertising, increasingly cluttered, typically produces low levels of trust, and in many categories fails to provide true product differentiation.

With the array of media choices increasing continually—think cable, the Internet, elevator ads—advertising messages now reach smaller and smaller audiences. Though many customer-loyalty programs have proven highly effective for the frequent business traveller, the same cannot be said for most other segments of the travel industry. Few families, for example, return to the same resort over and over again or take the same cruise more than once.

Advocacy-Focused Strategy

The challenge then presented by the dynamics in today's travel marketplace is to develop ways to strategically leverage the power of referrals on a grand scale, producing a demonstrable return on marketing investment. In an effective customer-referral strategy, for example, an experienced, satisfied guest informs friends and relatives not only about the great experience but also about nuts-and-bolts details about the travel firm's menu of services. This is accomplished by giving the satisfied guest some kind of "tool" to educate him/her properly. Such tools are designed to steer customer "advocates" toward relating their experiences not just with enthusiasm but with genuine knowledge as well.

This combination of facts-and-experience spurs customers to advocate not just once but again and again. We humans after all tend to trust our messengers. If even one friend, colleague, relative tells you she had a great time at a resort or on a cruise, you tend to believe her and will likely catch the fever for going out and experiencing this great getaway yourself! Consider how powerfully this "advertising message" might cut through the clutter and clamor of TV and radio commercials, Sunday circulars, junk mail, what have you.

Consider this success story: A cruise line had come to realize that, though customer advocacy played a pivotal role in its success as an industry leader, it nonetheless possessed no hard information on how critical it had been in terms of actual customer purchasing decisions or direct financial impact. Additionally, management decided (on a hunch) that the only ways to significantly increase advocacy were to either "bribe" customers by providing them with a monetary or credit incentives, or seek ways to make the cruise line's satisfied customers even more thrilled in hopes they would then share their "delight" with others.

Upon further reflection, however, neither option appeared very attractive. The first one, incentives, held the potential to undermine the company's premium brand position. Since the brand's foundation is built on the promise of "reliability," "integrity," "leadership" and "product innovation," it could be argued that bribing customers with an incentive would be at odds with the brand's core value. Encouraging advocacy via a monetary incentive might send the wrong message.

The second, the "customer delight" strategy, held limited appeal as well. Under this approach, the company's representatives would attempt to systemically exceed customers' service expectations, a strategy that sounded good in theory but in practice would surely increase costs per customer, perhaps to a level out of balance with potential returns. Then too was the risk that the many, now more, expensive "delighted customers" would still not bother to share their delightful experiences with others, despite added efforts on the part of the company.

So the company chose to investigate what other measurable, cost-effective methods it could employ to encourage customers to advocate its services. Its first step was to fully understand the value of an advocate. Based on previous industry research, they knew that:

— Receiving a recommendation from a customer advocate increased a prospect's purchase probability by 18 percent.

— On average, each advocate made three unique recommendations annually.

— The average purchase of those who had been advocated to was $650.

— As a result of the above, each advocate could be said to be worth approximately $400 in additional annual revenue.

— Further analysis revealed that an increase in the advocacy rate company-wide by only five percent would produce $240 million in new revenues.

With such data in hand, the company faced a challenge: Could it implement a strategy that systematically increased advocacy rates among its customer base? Also, how could it verify that such a strategic investment would be worth the effort?

To find out, a market research experiment was designed involving customers who had recently taken week long cruises. These purchasers were randomly assigned to a control or one of two test groups. Test Group A received a standard, off-the-shelf promotional-product type loyalty gift. Test Group B got a gift video designed to highlight and explain the uniqueness and value of the product. This inherent "customer education" subtly encouraged and "trained" the purchasers in Test Group B how to talk more knowledgeably about the product. Those in the control group received no post-purchase gift at all.

At the end of the three-month test period, research showed that the cruise company could expect dramatic differences in behaviour among the three groups. The control group showed no change from previous customer testing and Test Group A, the one that got the off-the-shelf gift, acted no different from the control group. However, Test Group B exhibited a remarkable increase in advocacy, demonstrating to the company that it could in fact proactively increase advocacy rates to great advantage. In terms of cost effectiveness, quantification of the purchase behaviour reported an 11-to-1 return on investment, and more than $2 million in additional advocate-driven sales emanating just from the small, second group, Test Group B. Needless to say, the company is now fully rolling out this new strategy.

Travel industry leaders have always recognized the value of referrals in generating new business but until recently there haven't been any known systemic ways to boost referrals. By strategically providing customers with real tools that both encourage and train them to act as advocates, however, travel marketers can be assured they will quantifiably increase customer advocacy, and dramatically. Customers who feel confident speaking more knowledgeably (and thus eloquently) about a travel experience will be more inclined to do so. This means the prospective customer, the one being advocated to, will find his/her purchase decision has been made easier as well.

Upon learning about a given resort or cruise or hotel from a trusted source, including positive, informed features and benefits, the prospect moves more quickly along the customer-conversion cycle, becoming first a new customer and later an excited advocate. When offered the right tools, our new customer advocate becomes a knowledgeable advocate as well, passing on information as well as excitement to many others and generating referrals beneficial to all.

Life-Safety Risks in Hospitality Industry

Despite the buffeting taken in the global economy in the last year international expansion for many hospitality companies will remain a necessity-not a choice. Hotel companies that do make the decision to "go global," as well as those already operating offshore, will benefit from addressing a key area of business risk-physical security and other life safety risks arising from various forms of workplace violence and other crime. International expansion mergers, deregulation and privatization often drive revenue growth, operational efficiencies and benefits to customers. But they can also be breeders of employee discontent, labor unrest, potential criminal disruption and terrorist actions. The U.S. State Department has reported that 75 percent of the 440 international terrorist acts in 1995 were directed against businesses. Fire safety is also a major area of risk and source of litigation for organizations around the world.

Because of these risks, hospitality organizations doing business in foreign markets should avoid the mistake of replicating the management models, construction design, security systems and training programs that work for them in their home countries. Just as risk must be carefully assessed in the marketing and financial arenas, hospitality companies also need rigorous risk "audits" when it comes to life safety systems and crisis management.

Questions for managers of international operations should include a range of questions.

- How much does our company know about the threats that can arise from criminal activity in regions or countries within which we operate?
- Are our security and life safety processes sufficient given the rise in threats to hotel properties in these destinations?

— Do these systems represent a comprehensive safeguard reflecting the realities of mobility and access to information in today's global community?

— How can we "design in" safety for our workforce and our guests?

To support work with hospitality organizations around the world, Arthur Andersen has developed an extensive computer database to help identify risks, assess probability of threats and assist in mitigating the potential for disasters. The database-which now encompasses 80 countries - tracks bombings, assaults, kidnappings, thefts, and other criminal acts committed by disgruntled employees, criminals and terrorists.

Drawn from government, business and news sources, the database contains information on 10 industries and 33 industry subgroups. "Hospitality and Leisure" data covers hotels, restaurants and tourism. Information from region to region, however, varies in depth because of the lack of a uniform reporting system. Law enforcement jurisdictions categorize events differently or do not maintain comprehensive counts. The database provides approximate totals, which are nevertheless revealing. The database is intended to make it possible to benchmark data in various parts of the world, particularly where information is generally incomplete or not systematically reported.

We begin by looking at regional totals in emerging markets for a collection of events that included bombings, hijackings, strikes / protests and sabotage. The database does not capture every event, and consequently the statistics should not be viewed as comprehensive. However, they do provide a picture emphasizing the need for attention to risk by hospitality industry managers. The following table shows an approximate number of incidents of bombings and attempted bombings, hijackings, kidnappings, strikes and protests, and a miscellaneous category of criminal acts for four regions of the world where global hospitality organizations have been expanding quickly in recent years.

Incidents of Criminal Activities

Region	1990-1998	1995-1998
Africa	418	344
Asia	956	781
Latin America	724	544
Middle East	204	160

An analysis of incidents worldwide suggests that the primary security threats arise from the following

Bombings

Most prevalent in all regions. In Africa, for example, there were 182 bombings or attempted bombings between 1990 and 1998, while Asia reportings showed a count of 358. Latin America at 344 and the Middle East at 119. Bombings typically result in extensive property damage, high incidence of injury and lengthy disruption of operations, not only to the target company, but to adjoining businesses extending blocks or miles from the bombing target. For example, Colombian authorities were able to foil a plot by guerrillas to detonate a car bomb at a hotel in Colombia. The hotel was the site of a major international banking conference, with guest speakers including the presidents of Colombia, Panama and Peru. The apparent motive was to show solidarity with guerrilla groups in Peru.

In April 1998, an international chain hotel, located in Uganda, was the target of a bombing resulting in five deaths. President Clinton had stayed in this hotel just four days before on his visit to Africa. Since January, Athens, the capital of Greece, has experienced over 150 bombings, directed at diplomatic facilities and foreign business establishments by a terrorist group trying to discourage foreigners from working or operating in Greece.

India has experienced a number of bombings during 1998. During October 1997, terrorists attempted to place a truck bomb at a five-star hotel in Colombo, Sri Lanka, but were stopped by hotel security from gaining entrance into the parking lot. The terrorist thereafter parked the vehicle near two other five-star hotels, detonating the device causing major damage to the hotels and surrounding buildings and killing eleven people and wounding 105. The hotels were located near government buildings.

Assaults

The second most frequent offenses reported after bombings. Not included on the earlier table because of the difficulty of capturing total data, assaults take the form of shootings, murder and physical assaults on a person. Various police jurisdictions report high numbers. According to Sao Paulo, Brazil police records, for example. 4,778 people were murdered in Sao Paulo in 1997, averaging 13 homicides per day. The Brazilian Ministry of Justice reported that 31 of every 100,000 Brazilians are murdered compared to 20 per 100,000 in Mexico and 10 per 100,000 in the United States. The records of the Colombian National Police reflected 31,808 murders or 87 per day in 1997, as well as 204 muggings or assaults committed in Colombia every 24 hours.

Mexico City reports more than 250,000 crimes annually or approximately 700 per day.

Kidnappings

This threat has emerged as a problem worldwide, reaching critical levels in Colombia and Mexico. Kidnappings are conducted by terrorists, criminals and others acting for political reasons. Most of the kidnappings are motivated by economic reasons, but in some cases are undertaken to effect political change in a country. Most are resolved peacefully, but some have tragic results.

Organized Crime

The threat from organized crime elements has reached global proportions. The threat ranges from the well-developed economies of the United States to such places as Hungary, Russia, India, South Africa and other emerging markets. Organized crime groups, sometimes working in concert with distant organizations, are generally engaged in transporting stolen goods internationally, extortion, murder, bombings, drug trafficking, arson and bribery of government officials. In Hungary, organized crime has been responsible for killing a diplomat, newspaper publisher, the bombing of several political candidates' houses and offices, as well as more than 100 other bombings since 1991.

Corruption

The International Monetary Fund, World Bank and Inter-American Development Bank are all addressing the issue as it relates to projects with which they are involved. The U.S. Commerce Department estimates that companies worldwide operating outside their own national borders, paid approximately $80 billion in illegal payments or bribes to officials in other countries since 1995. For an industry involved in operating buildings, the fact that corruption is extensive in the construction area should be of particular concern to hospitality managers. Where building inspectors are paid to overlook poorly constructed buildings or lack of compliance with building codes, there is a potential for disaster. Such activity has resulted in a number of incidents, including building collapses resulting in injury and death.

Clearly there are risks for hospitality companies "going global," particularly in markets where there is a history of political and economic instability. Hotel organizations frequently rely on security systems that are transplanted from property to property. But hospitality managers should consider a number of pertinent questions.

— When was the last complete security survey completed for all facilities?

— Is the system sufficient to the threats in the local area?

— Have new risks developed since the last surrey?

— Is there an effective emergency management plan in place?

— Will staff be proficient in its execution?

When reviewing threats in a country or region, it is important to focus not only on what directly appears to affect the hospitality industry, but also on the environment as a totality. A detailed security audit, combined with well-designed life-safety systems and training programs at individual properties, is essential. The following list might be regarded as a minimal risk assessment before venturing into many, if not most, markets outside one's home base of operations. Portions of the checklist also apply to undertaking security audits for hospitality properties planned or in operation in the home country:

In-Country Threat Assessment

Prior to physically launching operations, an analysis should be conducted of the country and of the market within which the hotel is located - whether it be a city or non - urban environment. In this process, current threats may be addressed in the immediate market area, as well as in the national context. As appropriate, such a review might also encompass adjacent communities and countries. The risk assessment should encompass the identification of particular criminal problems and crime statistics, as well as the evaluation of local and regional law enforcement agencies. The agency review should in particular focus on an assessment of proficiency. training, degree of professionalism and level of response to incidents. In conducting this review, enlisting the involvement of one's in-country embassy may also be helpful.

Physical Security Survey

Once the in-country and market area assessments are complete, the next step is a physical security survey. If done thoroughly at the outset, it may reduce the frequency of need for future assessments. Terrorism, for example, is currently a dominant concern in some environments, but the emphasis can shift quickly if the subject property becomes the target of guest room theft or assaults.

The common link here, however, is perimeter security and access control. Both of these issues should be addressed in the physical security survey. Such a review would not only consider the physical issues such as perimeter security and access control, but also the likely origins of the threat whether it be terrorist, criminal or labor related. The survey should include the identification of vulnerabilities and critical operational components, such as communica-tions. power supply and valuable storage and data processing areas. Furthermore, it should encompass assessment of access control points, perimeter security, alarms/CCTV, lighting and finally a detailed review of security procedures.

Building Design and Security

New construction should include a crime-prevention design audit. Design for crime prevention in hotel development can he highly beneficial. To be considered are such factors as the relationship of buildings to parking areas and structures, lighting, perimeter views and protection, and security systems.

Pre-Employment Screening/Training

All hotel employees should have a thorough background check conducted. There have been a number of instances in which hotels have hired individuals with criminal records in illegal drug sales or theft. Incidents of drug dealing. time-clock tampering and guest theft are relatively common problems that can be greatly mitigated with thorough employment and criminal checks. This process is especially important when selecting security personnel.

Training

These programs should be developed to enhance security among all hotel staff. in addition to the security force. Employee training should not only include a focus on hotel functions (guest relations. check-in procedures. daily operations, and administrative responsibilities). but security awareness as well. As is the case at most hotels. the security staff is limited and is sometimes strained due to commitments and shrinking staff. By providing the entire hotel staff with training in the identification of security issues, a description of operational methods, where to report information. and periodic updates on security advisories. management can in effect add additional "eyes" and ears to the organization.

Security Planning and Operations

It is important to broaden the focus of risk and systematize processes. Each hotel, for example. should have a detailed bomb threat plan that covers procedures to include:

1) the reporting person;
2) execution of the search plan;
3) what to do if a suspect package is found; and
4) evacuation plans.

The process is critical because time is always of the essence. Many bomb threats are made for the purpose of disrupting a company's operations. Needless evacuation of a facility can play into the hands of the person making the threat. On the other hand, information must be properly handled because of the scope of the potential damage.

Special Events Planning

These events often involve government dignitaries. officials and organizations, senior management. associations that may be embroiled in controversial policies. or business transactions that can elevate the security threat. In some cases. police or other government agencies provide security. but this does not obviate hotel responsibility. The example of the bomb threat at the banking conference in Colombia, for example. was augmented by exposure of detailed conference plans on the Internet. The hotel needs to track where information has been distributed, including the Internet, to determine the level of risk that may result.

Companies establishing new operations in other countries must begin by understanding the risks inherent in these locations. Taking "local knowledge" too much for granted can be costly. If an incident does occur, the consequences can be extraordinarily high. Compounding the threats to people and buildings are the prospects of financial loss. And yet the protection of insurance coverage should not reduce the sensitivity of hospitality managers to these risks, which can have completely unforeseen consequences. Negative publicity or litigation arising from such incidents can have an adverse effect on a company's reputation. stock price, employee morale and future business relationships.

By focusing on proactive safeguards, rather than reactive measures, hospitality companies can reduce risk efficiently and cost - effectively. The important point is not to wait until a major incident shatters the status quo. The time to assess risks and build security and crisis management systems is before-not after-an emergency.

6

Emerging Trends

Within this new economy, the operating environment for hospitality companies is changing. There are new rules of conduct, new relationships and new criteria for success, along with a new set of metrics. The revolution that we must now confront is therefore no less significant than the one that our forebears had to deal with as the industrial revolution changed how people lived, worked and dealt with each other. And like our distant relatives of centuries ago, there are boundless opportunities and countless risks, most obscured within an environment of great uncertainty. In such an era there are certain traits to business behavior that will distinguish success from failure. At this stage in the new economy's evolution, these traits would appear to include speed, agility and flexibility.

Speed is necessary to get to market early with a first-mover advantage that assures early adoption by an increasingly fickle, restless and frequently disloyal customer. Such speed is imperative as so-called "start-up" companies come to dominate their chosen niche in extremely short periods of time, frequently preempting the opportunity for those too slow to react.

Agility is required to be able to respond to competitive threats by not only those we know and can monitor, but also unseen competitors. These latter competitors may not even exist as yet, but as they emerge, they may quickly disintermediate established customer relationships.

And, finally, flexibility is needed to reorganize the established models of business and all of the related processes, and adapt the organization in organic fashion to a new environment in whatever form it takes.

For business executives at large, one of the most compelling changes that has confronted them in recent years is the potential for e-business. But while the significance of these new media are all too apparent, the business solutions required to capitalize on opportunities they offer are unfortunately not.

For most hospitality executives, the essential frame of reference has been a geocentric one where real estate and geography have been the big drivers in a physical world—buildings, dots on maps, markets served, chains. In tomorrow's world, these concepts will require some fundamental adjustments to provide for market "spaces" rather than "places" as the nature of relationships between hotel businesses, their customers, their suppliers and their alliance partners go through rapid and constant change.

As these changes occur, the new economy's business leaders must quickly learn the new rules of the game and adjust their approaches accordingly. And the most successful among us will align key processes around the Internet, build corporate intelligence automatically, create integrated value chains and develop new processes to deal with an ever-changing set of circumstances.

Supporting the changes in the new economy will be a vast pool of talented human capital anxious to bring new ideas and new technologies to bear on the traditional ways of doing business and, in doing so, steadily increase the pace of productivity improvement. And if the hospitality industry is to respond to this coming reality, it will need to address some of its most vexing challenges—particularly those relating to the recruitment, training and development of human capital. The human capital inventory for an e-business will require entrepreneurship, as well as visionary leadership, strength in sales and marketing and commitment to customer relationship management. The organizational bias will need to be toward creativity and risk-taking, and away from dependency on analysis and procedures.

In addition to the human capital challenge, many of today's legacy organizations are better structured to work in the old economy, but are considerably less aligned for many activities in the "new." The cultural challenges may in fact be no less daunting than those presented by some of the technological ones. For large organizations attempting a major shift in orientation, the presence of a significant culture may turn out to be quite a hindrance.

Redefining the Hospitality Business

In some industries, profits are made on spare parts and maintenance rather than on mainstream products. In the new economy, we may see this business model replicated in the hospitality industry. And for those companies that discount or give away products such as hotel rooms in order to sell linked services, they surely will be redefining the meaning of hospitality. They will also be marketing an array of hospitality and leisure products and services to a customer base that is no longer satisfied with the traditional ways of making such purchases.

Hospitality businesses that traditionally provided room, board, management and marketing may need to rethink their roles in the new economy, particularly as services become more valuable than products. With the rapid growth of "infomediaries" and their facilitation of transactions, hospitality businesses may need to redefine themselves in order to prosper in an increasingly electronic world where one-to-one customization is the order of the day. But for those contemplating repositioning their companies in an e-business environment, it will be necessary to focus on the current value proposition of the business and determine how it might be reformatted or enhanced to ensure success in the new setting.

But just how prepared is the global hospitality industry to capitalize on some of the opportunities afforded by the emerging new economy? In Arthur Andersen's recently published global survey of technology, Hospitality 2000: The Technology, we addressed some of the issues that the industry is facing. These included the closed nature of our technology architectures, the way in which we collect information on our customers, our investments in Internet, intranet and extranet technologies, and our adoption of electronic commerce.

The results are not especially encouraging and suggest an industry still relatively slow to adapt to e-business. Only 39% of the industry's Web sites, for example, can handle reservations on a real-time basis, and even fewer still (19%), collect customer information.

At the same time, just 22% are using "push" marketing programs and a distinct minority (just 19%), have extranets to suppliers or customers. But these adoption rates are nonetheless projected to grow and we should, therefore, expect our industry's leaders to be far more attuned to the needs of an e-business environment in the years to come.

As information technology (IT) is used to facilitate a company's entry into the world of electronic commerce, our industry's leadership will also need to overcome a natural tendency to be disappointed by the role of IT in achieving competitive advantage. For many years IT was seen as a mechanism to support back office finance and accounting functions. In the future, it inevitably will be one of the principal drivers of value creation in the new economy. But we should not be mislead by IT—in e-business, it will be the strategy, not the technology that will make the difference between success and failure. But having the strategy in place is only the first step. It must be linked to every part of the business.

PLANNING FOR E-BUSINESS

With the costs of playing in the e-business world escalating rapidly, hospitality executives should consider the four phases of what might be called the "E-Business Lifecycle." The first of these—E-Business Strategy Development and Planning—must address the market and competitive context, articulate the vision and opportunity, outline the strategy and the business case, and identify the risks. In recent years, we have frequently seen hospitality businesses put up a Web site on the Internet and consider this an e-business strategy. But without a strategy for this new form of commerce and the business planning process to drive it, such reactionary approaches stand little chance for success.

Once the plan is in place, an e-business design phase can commence to address site design, lay out the business architecture, identify the technical infrastructure, plan for performance, availability and capacity, and deal with tax issues and enterprise security. Following the design phase, E-Business implementation will prepare for the launch with training and change enablement, implementation and integration, testing and roll-out. Once in place, E-Business Operations will need to be supported by IT and audit services, Web site activity analysis and Web site maintenance. Finally, measurement systems will need to be established to monitor performance.

As industry executives embark on this e-business lifecycle, they will need in the first stage to clearly establish the business case for investing in new technologies, systems and organizations by addressing both the cost reduction and revenue enhancement benefits. On the revenue side, there are a number of factors to consider. These include the company's ability to identify and recruit the most valuable customers; the ability to seamlessly cross-sell the company's products and services, as well as those of alliance partners; the ability to retain valuable customers and reduce attrition (especially relevant in a world of questionable brand loyalty); and finally, when and how to eliminate costly and unnecessary discounts through revenue optimization.

In this kind of environment, the property management system will no longer hold sway as the center of the hospitality universe, but will become just one in a series of customer touch-points that will increasingly include the Internet. These touch-points will ultimately need to be fully integrated into a customer information system supported by sophisticated data warehousing and data mining technologies.

Adding to the industry's costs in this portrait of the future is the cost of grafting e-business technologies onto the industry's legacy systems. At a certain stage, it may make sense to start from scratch and ensure that every system is Web-enabled. This would allow a total interface for a high-growth e-business, thereby maximizing the customer relationship management opportunities that it presents.

As to the role of the Internet, its comprehensive reach and ubiquitous nature has already ensured its central place in the new economy. But how should we evaluate whether an Internet application is deserving of our attention? Firstly, productivity on the Internet in the years to come will be vastly improved by much higher bandwidth than is currently in place. And with higher bandwidth will come applications that can benefit from such extra capacity delivering tightly focused and reliable content to an increasingly sophisticated and demanding e-customer. If an Internet application is to succeed in the future, it will therefore need to be designed to capitalize on this coming reality.

Secondly, an Internet application needs to form a community of some sort because without a sense of place, albeit of the virtual sort participants will not have that all-important sense of belonging. And as with the industrial revolution, which drew a disparate population to centers of economic activity, so will such "intranet communities" grow in value as their populations increase in size and their economic product expands. For larger businesses that form such communities, they are developing new revenue sources and are reinventing their relationships with customers, employees, suppliers and partners. Smaller companies intent on participating in this new environment, may need to be content as a participant in an established community, rather than trying to take on the creation of a community itself. It is better, perhaps, to be one of many players in a successful space than struggling to establish an identity in a world surrounded by also-rans.

Whether large or small, community developers and marketers of the virtual sort will have to recognize that what may have appeared cool in the physical world to generations brought up in the old economy will not work in the world of e-business. Being cool and staying that way in order to get and keep attention will remain a constant challenge, especially for those keen to nurture a younger generation of travelers brought up on MTV and the Web.

Finally, the successful Internet application needs to improve service while reducing transaction costs, particularly as the balance of power in the buy/sell relationship continues its inexorable migration from sellers to buyers. Service improvement strategies will be nothing new for hospitality businesses, but it is noteworthy that service (rather than on-time delivery, price or other concerns) is the top factor that encourages return e-business. This must be an area of focus since the current growth of e-business appears destined to outpace the supporting infrastructure and its related service at least over the short term. But as hospitality executives know, delivering good service can be expensive. Scaling the types of service response to the circumstances is a growing need, but one that can be modulated if the value of each customer can be distinguished and the response adjusted accordingly. In considering the opportunities in hospitality e-business, industry leaders should take stock of the dynamics that are occurring in the new economy and plan accordingly. It is probably easy to dismiss the e-business world as a playground for others with products and services that are more obviously applicable. But our industry is changing, as is the world around us.

Human Resources of Hospitality Industry

The hospitality industry has traditionally focused much of its attention on the assets it best understands - real property and the capital that finances it. And yet what will distinguish the most successful companies of the next century will be the effective management of people, information and customer relationships - the industry's intangible assets. Today's industry leaders are therefore challenged to develop the tools which will measure, manage and influence these intangible assets as they contribute increasingly to the value of business enterprises.

In dealing with this challenge, our industry's leadership must consider an array of issues confronting the people side of our business - the methods for learning more about our customers - and how we recruit, train and develop our employees. To address these and other issues, Arthur Andersen and New York University launched the second in a series of landmark global surveys of the hospitality industry's leadership, Hospitality 2000 - The People. This research provides for the first time a comprehensive view of those factors that will contribute to the successful management of the industry's human capital resources in the year 2000 and beyond. Following a broad literature search, focus group discussions, and best practice benchmarking, a comprehensive questionnaire survey was sent to hospitality industry executives around the world. Close to 500 responses from executives in the Americas, Asia / Pacific and Europe, the Middle East, India and Africa (EMEIA) have now been tabulated and analyzed and will be published along with best practice case studies of major hospitality companies in the final report. An overview of critical findings of the research follows.

Developing the Customer Relationship

While much of the survey focused on the management of employees or "human capital," attention was also paid to the customer and how the relationship is measured in terms of satisfaction, loyalty and value. There is a certain irony in the fact that the industry's customers spend more time with us than with most providers of products and services, yet we know very little about them and more importantly how they feel about us.

As anticipated, most respondents (89 percent) indicated continued use of guest comment cards left in hotel rooms - a practice that clearly does not produce a valid measurement of customer satisfaction. Their use, however, will decline by as much as one-third by the year 2000, to be replaced with more sophisticated approaches to measuring customer satisfaction. In fact, a surprisingly high proportion of respondents currently use research techniques such as telephone surveys (18 percent) and formal surveys during guest stays (35 percent). Electronic surveys upon checkout, which hold much promise for rapid feedback and analysis. are in wider use in the Americas (16 percent). than elsewhere (3 percent). Their use, however, will increase more than four-fold in the future - 43 percent against 10 percent overall today.

In the future, we can expect this process of information gathering to become far more sophisticated and expansive as investments in technology provide for data warehousing, customer valuation and efficient "one-to-one marketing. In the meantime, a surprisingly high proportion of respondents report collecting spending (57 percent) and life-style (27 percent) information.

Table 1. How do organizations measure customer satisfaction?

	1997	2000
Formal Telephone Survey	18%	22%
Formal Survey during stay	35%	38%
Guest Comment Cards	89%	62%
Focus Groups	26%	39%
One-to-one interviews	28%	34%
Electronic form at check-out	10%	43%
No information collected	2%	0%
No answer	1%	9%

Developing a Strategy

Many respondents identified human resources (HR) as an important feature of long-term planning and nearly three-quarters felt their human resource practices, policies and procedures were aligned with their overall business strategy. As to the impact of technology, opinion was evenly split as to whether it will reduce the number of general staff required in the future, although there were some important differences regionally. In Asia / Pacific, close to two-thirds felt that technology would have this impact. In contrast, just one-third in the Americas said this would be the case. Most respondents (89 percent) agreed that technology will necessitate a change in the skills people require. And many more agreed than disagreed that technology could improve job motivation (36 percent compared to 16 percent) and job satisfaction (48 percent to 12 percent).

The role of HR management is not always clear in today's hospitality companies. In our research, we tried to clarify the industry's view by asking our respondents to categorize their HR management. One-third decided that HR managers were administrative types, while 21 percent preferred the "Business Partner" moniker. "Strategic Partner" was agreed to by 18 percent, while only 14 percent picked "Employee Champion." And trailing in last places were "Line Manager" (11 percent) and "Change Agent" (9 percent). As to the future view, we were pleased to learn that "Administrative Expert" was dropped by most (34 percent today down to 11 percent), offset by a big increase in the "Strategic Partner" designation (18 percent today up to 49 percent in the future). Clearly the human resource function of the future will have a more bottom-line business orientation than it has had in the past. For this transition to be effective, however, a greater alignment of human capital management with the core business strategy will be required, coupled with more sophisticated measurements of performance.

While the human resource function gets redefined within the organization, its component parts are on offer without. Increasingly popular as a tool for more effective business management, outsourcing appears destined to make in-roads into the HR function, part of a larger trend toward increased use of specialized vendors and other partners. In the future, we can expect to see more HR functions outsourced with one-third of respondents seeing training and benefits administration as outsource candidates for their organizations in the future (up 25-30 percent over today).

As those with responsibility for the industry's human capital ponder the future, they should consider the priorities that our respondents have emphasized. Presented with a list of 17 human capital resource issues, we asked our respondents to list the top priorities for the future - and they were quite clear where these priorities should lie - it is in having a customer focus, with satisfied employees who are prepared for change.

Recruitment and Retention Challenge

Though sound recruitment planning is critical to the establishment of adequate human resources within the industry, only 64 percent of respondents reported having a recruitment plan in place - and 40 percent of these plans extended for only one year.

This relatively low level of planning appears to contradict the assertion that human resource concerns are being aligned with business planning. In the absence of a solid recruitment plan, hiring can only be reactive - a less than desirable practice given the industry's problem with high turnover and the ever-increasing competition for qualified labor from better-paying industries.

Recruiting people to our industry is unfortunately only one of today's human capital challenges. Employee retention appears to be just as big a headache and it may get worse before it gets better. To counter this, approximately two-thirds of respondents plan an array of strategies, including the increased use of incentive pay, more job enrichment programs, improved working conditions, improved screening tools and increases in benefits.

Once recruited, a number of strategies are used to reduce employee turnover - some effective, others less so. Improving the work environment, sharing information and increasing employee involvement in decision making are some of the leading choices. And as if to say that money isn't everything, base pay was suggested by only 50 percent of our respondents as an effective strategy to mitigate employee turnover.

This suggests, however, that the hospitality industry may continue to find itself at a disadvantage when competing for qualified employees with better-paying industries.

In looking at what contributes the most to employee turnover, there does not appear to be an overwhelmingly strong view in favor of any one factor. In order of significance, they were compensation, hours of work, opportunity for employment in other industries, benefits, work conditions, internal opportunity for growth and finally the image of the industry itself.

Table 2. Shortage of labor in Hospitality Industry

	Overall	EMEAI	Americas	Asia/ Pacific
Agree	74%	62%	81%	82%
Disagree	11%	15%	9%	8%
Neither Agree Nor Disagree	13%	21%	9%	10%
Don't Know / No Answer	2%	1%	1%	
Total	100%	100$	100%	100%

Table 3. Issues contributing to the shortage of qualified labor in the hospitality industry

	Total Agree	EMEAI Agree	Americas Agree	Asia / Pacific Agree
Competition from better paying industries	78%	74%	81%	74%
Low compensation levels	67%	60%	73%	54%
Low acceptance of service culture	5%	66%	56%	54%
Industry image	44%	53%	39%	33%
Inadequate hospitality education	42%	44%	37%	54%
Poor growth opportunities	29%	31%	29%	21%

Trends of Brand Marketing

In the wake of the huge expansion of the last decade, an abundance of brands gained a tenuous foothold in the marketplace as the segmentation fostered by our industry's leaders generated a proliferation of newcomers. Many of these brands have struggled to build a sense of identity, and their futures remain in limbo. To the owners and lenders who provide capital to the hospitality industry worldwide, the issue of brand identity has taken on a new and important meaning. Decisions concerning the approach to brand marketing frequently define the difference between an organization's success or failure, and these questions are getting more rigorous attention than ever before. And if investors and lenders are sometimes confused about what's at stake, consider the confused consumer, buffeted by the mixed brand signals he frequently gets from the industry. It is thus legitimate to ask whether brand marketing in the hospitality sector involves more art than science.

Conventional wisdom suggests that the hotel industry is consolidating with an increasing portion of the world's hotels affiliated with chains, as opposed to remaining independent. In the United States, for example, approximately 70 percent of hotel properties are "chain-affiliated," and it is assumed that the customer increasingly prefers accommodations that fly a flag a kind of "good housekeeping" sign of approval. Despite the flagging of property, however, consumer research suggests that a steady minority of travelers remain evidently quite satisfied with non-branded products approximately 28 percent of leisure travelers and 22 percent of business travelers.

During the 1980s, the hotel industry saw an explosion of new brands, most particularly in the ultra-competitive U.S. marketplace, but also in several countries in Europe, including the United Kingdom and France. Stymied either by the real estate crash of the early 1990s or simply a casualty of poor strategic brand visioning, many of these brands never achieved the required critical mass to flourish. As a consequence, a multitude of names continue to struggle for the customer's attention, some of which cannot compete as national or even regional brands. Furthermore, in a globalizing marketplace, national brand presence itself may not be sufficient for success in the future.

Market segmentation has served as one of the most powerful drivers in the creation of more and more branded products a trend that became a popular marketing concept in the 1980s and remains so today. Seen as a vehicle for growth by a number of hotel companies that tapped a virtually limitless supply of capital in those years, the new products sliced and diced the hotel market in a continuing quest for increased market share. Large hotel chains assumed that they could create new markets by establishing niche products in a variety of segments. With the benefit of hindsight, however, some of this thinking was probably shortsighted. It is fair to say that while overall demand was growing during those years, the reality was that many newly created brands were stealing market share - sometimes from the chain's own customers.

Some hotel chains that started out in a mid-market segment have tried to move up-market by creating new brand concepts to do so. Holiday's Crowne Plaza and Ramada's Renaissance represent examples. At the same time, upscale chains created more moderate brands to broaden their coverage of the market. Experience with both strategies has by now suggested that moving up-market is more difficult than going down-market.

As hotel companies fine-tune their identities, reposition their products and promote growth through aggressive franchising programs, owners and operators are frequently quite indecisive about how to apply a brand strategy to the marketing of their property. The result - a great deal of flag changing at individual properties as repositioning strategies following change of ownership or renovation encourage the switching from one flag to another. Hotels also switch from independent status to a flag and back again with great alacrity. In the United States such movements account for as many as 300 to 400 instances of re-flagging of each type annually. No wonder the customer becomes confused! This volatility has tended to erode brand loyalty - perhaps one of the most pressing challenges for the industry today.

Customers Drive Shareholder Wealth

Marketing executives have historically marshaled their efforts in determining how to best create and then sustain brand loyalty. The larger question of critical importance today, however, is the relationship of brand value to the accretion of shareholder wealth. In reality, capital markets value branded companies with loyal customers more highly than property companies that have little identity or customer following.

In a chaotic world with fragile customer loyalties and fast shifting market preferences, those companies focusing on brand development driving it with dedicated customer support - will probably be the winners in the future. This involves a fundamental shift in perspective. The customer becomes the primary asset, not the fixed asset known as a hotel. The hotel "box" becomes part of the distribution system - a system that delivers branded products and services to the customer. In the globalized markets of the future, *the customer will be king*. Thus the brand becomes a focus for the company and a rallying call in the marketplace.

Branded products and services, then, will become an even more important part of the marketing landscape in the future. Those companies that control well-recognized brands will be well-rewarded by higher than average returns and capital market support that values such customer focus. This raises the question of how the industry's leading companies will proceed in their efforts to promote brands globally.

Some companies that own multiple brands have attempted to market all of their brands in an integrated message whereas others have focused on each brand separately. There are clearly advantages to both strategies

- the "glow effect" of one strong brand supporting its weaker sisters in the case of the former and the focused segmentation approach, allowing brands of differing quality to be positioned separately in the case of the latter.

Brands, to be effective, must be promoted through the mass media. But advertising in the media has become a very expensive proposition as the "noise level" increases and the channels of distribution continue to expand along with the revolution in communications.

As a result, we can expect to see less money being spent on advertising in the future and more on direct and highly focused marketing to identified customers. This, of course, will need to be driven by sophisticated customer tracking systems that tie into the way in which reservations are made and customers arrive and depart from the hotels that they stay in.

But brand loyalty can be extremely difficult to achieve and thus for some, it is a loyalty that must be bought. Nothing is more symptomatic of this proposition than the frequent traveler program - a marketing concept introduced into the hotel industry following its incarnation in the airline business. In both industries, it is by now viewed by many as an expensive luxury that cannot be afforded. In spite of this, we continue to see vast sums of money being spent in support of such programs.

Technology

In the hospitality industry, as in all arenas of commerce, technology represents one of the strongest forces for change, while having had a significant impact on brand marketing. Hotel reservation systems have been shifting from voice to electronic Global Distribution Systems and are now on the verge of consumer access via the Internet.

The increasing role played by the Internet should slowly affect booking patterns in the future as inexpensive consumer access to hotel product becomes available. This, of course, has potential implications for the benefits associated with the branding of hospitality products. On the plus side, global communications that bring branded products and services closer to the customer should encourage wider recognition.

On the negative side, if hotel products can be accessed visually and directly by distant consumers, the presumed uniformity of standards under today's brand identities will be more closely scrutinized as customers' buy decisions are being made. At that point, brands will then have to deliver what they promote - something that is not always the case in the today's market. And as for the definition of a "marketplace" in tomorrow's electronic world - it will clearly have become the "marketspace."

As this evolution continues, technology can serve as an important ally for hotel organizations building brand identity. Business managers generally spend a great deal of time monitoring awareness and advertising effectiveness. In the hospitality sector, it is probably fair to say that a relatively poor job is being done in this regard.

Technology provides an essential tool for hotel organizations to keep a hand on the pulse of customer wants and needs. Systems must be designed that allow hotel brand managers to closely track their customers and potential customers - monitoring behavioral patterns and responses to the products and services that are being delivered. Much too little of this is being done in the hospitality industry. We generally do a good job on an ex post basis of knowing where we have been.

Occupancy and average room rate statistics and historical financial results are produced in volume and in detail, but truly understanding who are the customers, what they think and do, when they do it and why are much more elusive. These are the challenges for brand managers today, and they will become that much more important to success in the future.

Franchising the Strengths

Franchising as a business seems to have achieved more respectability in the hotel industry than ever before as some franchised brands command noticeable leads in terms of awareness, product strength and value. While franchising historically has been associated with budget and mid-market brands, it is now being used with increased frequency to expand more upscale brands. Previous concerns relating to the difficulty of controlling wayward hotel owners and operators, who are not maintaining the higher standards expected in the upscale end of the business, have been mitigated by improvements in the organization of franchise support systems and the increasing volume of excellent independent management companies.

While franchising expands the presence of brand marketing in the international hospitality industry, the pure hotel management business is under increasing pressure as fees decline in the face of the competition for contracts. It appears that the industry increasingly views management more as a commodity than a unique set of skills that must be sought with great care. This trend is being driven by the fact that the industry's management skills have advanced dramatically during the last decade.

As chains expanded with their sophisticated operating systems, they spawned countless smaller independent management enterprises. These were launched by expatriates of these larger organizations and brought sophistication and well-proven techniques to a variety of hotel owners who saw value in associating with smaller management firms. In allying with such independent management companies, the marketing challenge has generally been "solved" by associating with a brand through a franchise relationship.

When there were fewer brands in the business than there are today, the pricing of franchised products and services was generally quite uniform even though what the franchisors delivered was not. Today, however, we see a more tailored approach to pricing, with much wider variation in pricing models driven more by the relative strength of the individual systems. This is a positive trend since it will produce a closer matching of results with customer (owners' and operators') expectations.

Brand Strategies & Marketing

Hotel owners and independent managers play an important role in deciding on the brand strategy to be pursued by individual properties. We often see managers of hotel properties change their brand affiliation in the search for a more productive reservation system.

To some, the production of a branded reservation system and the impact on average room rate are the acid tests of what works and what doesn't. Other attributes of a brand are perhaps just as relevant - consistency, sales office support, the matching of the brand's positioning with the property's optimum segment mix, image, future development plans on a system-wide basis and the impact of additional brand development in the local marketplace are some of the other factors to be considered. Understanding the total dynamic at work in selecting the optimum brand is a complex task that thus requires careful analysis.

A marketing plan, like any business plan, must address three components - strategy, organization and capital. Strategy outlines the vision for the future; organization addresses the people requirements, the skills and the processes; and finally capital deals with how financial resources can be deployed and what return they can expect.

In brand marketing, these areas are especially relevant in view of the large amounts of capital that tend to be deployed in the constant search for the customer and in the efforts to develop and retain customer loyalty. As hotel owners and operators consider the competitive dynamics of tomorrow's marketspace, they will need to plan fully if their brand strategies are to deliver on the promise of customer access and loyalty.

Product consistency, as a result, remains one of the most critical issues in the hotel industry. For new brands that were launched in the 1980s and have reached critical mass, there appears to be little difficulty in establishing product consistency, especially when most of the product is new construction and involves smaller, more simply engineered properties.

Other brands that rely on converting older facilities have frequently had difficulties, typically when they are under pressure to build up a chain quickly to reach critical mass. Balancing the demands for growth in a global brand-oriented marketplace with the desire for product integrity and consistency will always be a tough challenge. The outlook for those companies still struggling with product inconsistency remains somewhat cloudy.

A salvation for such companies in the past has been a strong development environment in which there is plenty of new construction. Since another development cycle is unlikely to be financed in the near future, inconsistent brand portfolios will become the repository for those properties that cannot afford to pay for higher-valued brands that in turn demand adherence to a core mission satisfying and exceeding customer expectations concerning the product they buy.

Given these complex factors, we again pose the question Is brand marketing in the hospitality industry more an art than a science? There is little question that brand marketing has been lacking in " science" historically. With little understanding of the customer - the who, the how, the what and the where - many brands were established purely as growth vehicles for companies that relied on other people's capital to expand.

As capital becomes more discerning in the future and as the customer becomes the primary focus of attention, this will inevitably change. Technology's impact will also force and support the move towards making brand marketing the science that it must become to support the successful hotel organizations of the next century.

Mass Customization in the Hospitality Industry

Mass production as a paradigm of management has dominated the world industrial production since World War II, and it has fettered the tremendous growth in American economy in the twentieth century. With shifting demographics and changing consumer tastes and preferences, mass production for homogeneous markets is not enough to keep businesses going.

In the present business world, organizations are facing tremendous forces to change to stay ahead of competitors. The companies that responded properly and quickly to changes are now beginning to master a new frontier in business competition. These companies found that not only can higher quality yield lower costs, but so can greater variety. In 1993, Pine stated that:

> "Customers can no longer be lumped together in a huge homogeneous market, but are individuals whose individual wants and needs can be ascertained and fulfilled. Reducing life-cycles and fragmenting demand can yield powerful advantages. Leading companies have created processes for low-cost, volume production of great variety, and even for individually customized goods and services. They have discovered the new frontier in business competition: Mass Customization."

Mass customization is arising in direct response to the turbulence that has splintered the mass market. One sharp-eyed observer who spotted the coming of mass customization long ago is perhaps United States' best known futurist, Alvin Toffler. As far back as 1970, Toffler wrote in Future Shock about "destandarized" goods and services that he forecast the United States would produce in "great variety." Speaking recently to INC by telephone, Toffler said that mass customization will proceed with a kind of gravitational force because, as American become more affluent, they have wanted greater individuality. People now can afford it partly because technology makes it cheaper. Michael Cox, chief economist at the Federal Reserve Bank of Dallas, in concurrence with Toffler lamented that "If you don't customize, you're going to lose business in today's marketplace."

Nowadays, virtually all companies recognize the need to be customer driven by providing superior service to satisfy customers' needs. But as customers and their needs grow increasing diverse, unnecessary cost and complexity are inevitably added to operations.

Companies around the world have embraced mass customization in an attempt to avoid those pitfalls of trying to meet every customer's need. Readily available information technology and flexible processes permit them to customize goods or services for individual customers in high volumes and at a relatively low cost.

Concepts of Mass Customization

Definitions

Mass customization is neither a simple strategy to undertake organizationally and operationally, nor is it a simple concept to comprehend. Hart defined mass customization by using two distinct definitions:

— *The visionary definition*: The ability to provide customers with anything they want profitably, any time they want it, anywhere they want it, any way they want it.

— *The practical definition*: The use of flexible processes and organizational structures to produce varied and often individually customized products and services at the low cost of a standardized, mass production system.

According to Hart, the goal in the first definition will rarely be achieved by an organization. It was considered a transcendent, absolute idea that exists solely as an ideal. The goal in the second definition is not the "anything-at-any-time" promised by the visionary definition.

It is "to ascertain, from the customer's perspective, the range within which a given product or service can be meaningfully customized (i.e. differentiated) for that customer, and then to facilitate the customer's choice of options from within that range." He lamented that the concept of producing tailor-made or partially tailor-made goods or services according to customer desire, with very short cycle times and mass production efficiencies, is a more realizable goal than that offered by the visionary definition.

In essence, mass customization is a hybrid technique by which a company churns out products in typical assembly-line fashion yet can add unique features to individual orders. This requires a flexible manufacturing system that anticipates a wide range of options.

However, due to the vast differences in customer preferences, mass customization, too, can produce unnecessary cost and complexity. Therefore, it is crucial that managers must examine thoroughly what kind of customization their customers would value before they adopt this new strategy.

Decision factors

Hart further identified four key decision factors:

1. *Customer sensitivity*. The first question companies need to ask themselves is: Do your customers care whether you offer more customization? If the answer is no, the mass customization potential is limited.

2. *Process amenability*. This is a multifaceted area. The first obvious question is: Does your process technology, which exists in your area allow you to customize your product or service to individual customers? If it does, the next question is how extensive an overhaul is required to incorporate this technology into your existing process and how much investment will be required?

   Another part of process amenability is marketing. Since the goal of mass customization is products or services tailored to individual customers, an important question for companies to ask is: Does the marketing department have access to the level of detail regarding customer needs and the capacity to analyze such information? A third consideration is design. Is your company capable of translating custom needs into actual specifications? The last consideration under this factor is production and distribution. Partly depending on the form and nature of product or service, the flexibility of the production system to handle mass customization is a critical point here.

3. *Competitive environment*. The major question here is: Are there competitive forces that would enhance or detract from the advantage your company would gain from implementing mass customization? In other words, would you be the first in your market with a

mass-customized product? How long would it take for competitors to react? And how will your competitors' customers react?

4. *Organizational readiness*. The last decision factor requires an honest assessment of your company's culture and resources. Is your company able and ready to capitalize on the opportunity inherent in mass customization? Organizational change requires enlightened leadership, open-minded management, and financial resources. Hence, mass customization strategy is unique to the company developing and implementing it. There is no "cookie-cutter" approach to creating such a strategy. Mass customization strategy that works for one company might not work for another company.

Approches to Mass Customization

In 1997, Gilmore and Pine identified four distinct approaches to customization, which are collaborative, adaptive, cosmetic, and transparent. They advocated that when designing or redesigning a product, process, or business unit, managers should choose an approach or a mix of some or all of the four approaches to serve their own particular set of customers.

1. *Collaborative customization*. This approach follows three steps: first to conduct a dialogue with individual customers to help them articulate their needs; second, to identify the precise offering that fulfills those needs; and third, to make customized products for them. Collaborative customization is most appropriate for businesses whose customers cannot easily articulate what they want and grow frustrated when forced to select from a plethora of options.

2. *Adaptive customization.* Adaptive customizers offer one standard, but customizable, product that is designed so that users can alter it themselves. This approach is appropriate for businesses whose customers want the product to perform in different ways on different occasions, and available technology makes it possible for them to customize the product easily on their own.

3. *Cosmetic customization.* This approach is appropriate when customers use a product the same way and differ only in how they want it presented. in other words, the standard offering is packaged specially for each customer.

4. *Transparent customization.* This approach is appropriate when customers' needs are predictable or can easily be deduced, and especially when customers do not want to state their needs repeatedly. Offerings were customized within a standard package for individual customers.

To sum up, collaborative customizers change the product itself in addition to changing some aspect of the presentation while a cosmetic customizer changes only the presentation of the product. A transparent customizer uses a standard representation to mask the customization of the product and finally adaptive customizers change neither the product nor the representation of the product but they provide the customer with the ability to change both the product's function and/or its presentation to meet their needs.

Pioneers of mass customization

It is important to look beyond the hospitality industry for ways to mass customize products and services in order to learn from other industries. Based on literature review, the following section discusses how some companies in the hospitality industry, as well as other industries mass customized their products and services. First, let's examine a few specific companies and see how they shifted from mass production to mass customization. They are summarized in Table 4.

Table 4. Examples of Paradigm Shift

Companies	Mass customization approach
Dell Computer	Dell Computer uses the collaborative approach and assembles computers to customer's exact specifications. In 1998, Dell sells around 6 million US dollars worth of built-to-order PCs a day. Dell passed IBM in early 1998 to claim the second spot in PC market share.
British Airways	The London-based airline plans to deliver top-notch customer service to its first-class frequent flyers through streamlining its supply-chain process. Understanding passengers' needs beforehand makes it possible for BA to deliver individualized items for passengers on each flight just before takeoff.
Ritz-Carlton	Ritz-Carlton uses software to personalize guests' experience by linking to database filled with quirks and preferences of half a million guests. Any bellhop or desk clerk can find out whether a guest is allergic to feathers, their favorite newspaper, or whether they like extra towels. The company stores guest information in a database and uses it to tailor the service to each guest on his/her next visit. This is a way to transparently customize for those customers who do not want to be bothered with direct collaboration.
Planters Company	Planters chose cosmetic customization when it retooled its old plant in Suffolk, Virginia. As an example, Wal-Mart wanted to sell peanuts

	and mixed nuts in larger quantities and 7-Eleven did. In the past, Planters could produce only long batches of small, medium, and large cans giving customers only these few standard packages which may not meet their requirements. Today, Planters can quickly switch between sizes, labels, and shipping containers, responding to each retailer's desires on an order-to-order basis.
Regent, Hong Kong	In the fine dining restaurant, the hotel cosmetically customizes paper napkins and matchbox by printing their customers' name on them. Although personalizing a service in this way is cosmetic, it is of value to many customers.
Lutron Electronics	Lutron's customers can adapt its lighting systems to maximize productivity at the office or to create appropriate moods at home without having to experiment with multiple switches each time they desire a new effect. The customer can quickly achieve the desired effect by punching in the programmed settings.
ChemStation	ChemStation produces industrial soap after independently analyzing each customer's needs. It formulates the right mixture of soap for each customer, which goes into a standard tank. The company learns each customer's usage pattern and delivers more soap before the customer has to ask. This approach eliminates the need for reordering. This is the transparent approach since the customer does not know which soap formulation they have or how much is in inventory but they know the soap works and is always there when they need it.

Fast-Food

Now, let's look more closely into how the hospitality industry mass customized products and services. Much has been said about the standardizing forces of

McDonaldization in the wider society . Fast-food restaurants and other McDonaldized systems are mass production systems, which were built upon the belief that in the world of mass production, consumers accept homogeneous products. Their acceptance facilitates market growth and the reduction of prices through economies of scale, which in turn leads to a greater price gap between mass-produced goods and that of customized goods.

As with other mass producers, the fast-food industry has reached the limited of the old paradigm. In 1995, Taylor and Lyon reported mass customization as an alternative to McDonaldization. They recognized that fast-food companies, including McDonald's, have experienced the same sources of discontinuity as other mass producers, creating extreme pressure for change. Burger King was the first one to embrace the principles of mass customization - "Have it your way!" and "Sometimes you've gotta break the rules!" The focus then was on burgers and fries but later shifts testified that this was only the start.

Using McDonald's as an example, it can be seen that standardization is still a characteristic of its operations. However, its menu has been expanded not only to suit local tastes and preferences but also to offer more variety. Pizza, fajitas, breakfast burritos, submarine sandwiches, spaghetti and meatballs, carrot and celery sticks were included in some menus. Internationally, for McDonald's in France the menu is written in three to five different languages, usually, French, German, Italian, Belgian, and Japanese. Some menu items, which are offered in France, are not available in the United States. These items are bagels, red seasoned potato wedges with dipping sauce, cakes and pastries, scones and croissants. The drinks offered are also different. Dr. Pepper and root beer are not offered while Orangina, an orange flavored carbonated drink, beer and wine are available for purchase. For the breakfast menu, McDonald's in France also offers a fruit salad and scones. Salad and dessert choices are also varied, as the chef salad is served with salmon and shrimp, and eclairs, brownies, muffins, and beignets are included in the dessert menu. Pork is not used in Muslim nations. Big Macs in India are prepared with mutton. Soups are offered in Hong Kong operations. Beverage cup sizes are much smaller in Asian countries' McDonald's, and there is no refill. One may argue that this is product differentiation, but why do we differentiate product? To suit customers' needs! For McDonald's to have radically expanded it output variety, it underwent a paradigm shift characterized by shorter development and production cycles, flexibility, autonomy, process innovations and the adoption of a true customer focus.

Lodging

Hospitality industry has generally preferred to keep wages low, thus avoiding the need for technological innovation, particularly in the actual delivery of its services. Although technology has been used extensively in a supporting role to enhance performance and effectiveness, (e.g., computer reservation system, air control technology, accounting system) there has been a great reluctance to replace human service providers with technologically driven alternatives. However, in recent years, some "tinkering" of mass customization has occurred in selected areas in the lodging industry. Some examples are summarized in Table 5. As seen from these examples, mass customization is made possible by technological applications.

Table 5. Some Examples of Mass Customization in Hotels

Area	Example
Rooms	Auto-Wake
Front Office	Flexible Self check-in, Self-check Folio Review, Self check-out
In-room Entertainment	Video (PPV, On-demand), Video games/ Casino Games, Internet Connectivity
In-room Vending	Honor Bar, Micro-Based Dispensing
Guest Information Systems	In-Room Information Links

Could you ever imagine selling guest rooms that customers could personally customize, down to their favorite wall art, prior to check-in? The hotel guest room of the future project, sponsored by Conrad N. Hilton College at the University of Houston, is developing ideas to assist hoteliers' globally to mass customize the hotel product to better meet individual customer's need by mastering technological change.

The premise of this project is that a hotel guest room should be divided into zones that include work, entertainment and relaxation/rest; technology can then be introduced into each zone that enhances the guest's satisfaction. The project believes that technologies must be considered which impact upon: ergonomics, temperature, light, sound, exercise and diet; and variation of such technology that are responsive to the guest's principle purpose for using the room, work or leisure or a combination of both; and also consider the physiological, psychological and sociological needs of the guests.

There have been ample discussions about the aging global population and its implications for future marketing strategies and service provisions. This new demographic trend suggests new features in the hotel room that caters specifically to the needs and preferences of the senior travelers.

These new features, made possible by technology include:

— *ergonomically-designed furniture* that facilitates standing from a seated position with the aid of a weight/height sensing cushion or provides support to a tired back through sensors that adjust to the most comforting back support;

— *blankets* that utilize the same fiber technology as found on the space shuttles heat shield and thus will respond to body temperature retaining or expelling heat to maintain a comfortable temperature and more restful night's sleep;

— *alarm clocks* that awaken the guest to increasing light levels that begin with the light daybreak to a full daylight, for those whose hearing may riot be as sharp as it was in the past.

The applications of virtual reality are also a unique feature of the future hotel room. The project is examining the applications of video walls that would replace or perhaps supplement windows in guest rooms, allowing the room's occupant to select the scenery that would be most complimentary to her/his activity in the room.

For the business traveler in the work zone it might be sights and sounds that are most stimulating to the busy executive's productivity, transferring to the entertainment zone with sights and sounds from his/her favorite sporting event or concert; and finally to the relaxation/rest zone, where the stress business traveler can unwind with the sight/sounds of family or a favorite vacation spot.

With all that is said about high-tech, the bottom line is that guests want a room that is comfortable and adaptable to their particular needs. Many guests' expectations are not particularly high-tech. All guests want a good night's sleep which may mean paying attention to the soundness of the mattress being provided: what type of mattress does you guest prefer?

According to the Westin sleep study conducted for the chain by a New York-based research firm, the main criticism by 27% of respondents was that hotel mattresses are too soft. For another 21 percent, the number one complaint was that mattresses are too hard. There are two concepts - one utilizing springs and the other air -are being studied that will allow guests to adjust the firmness of each side of a bed. Other than the mattresses, guest of the future hotel room will be provided an assortment of pillows ranging from soft to firm and some or all hypoallergenic.

Industries, which are less dependent on the human interactions have adopted laborsaving technology. As a result, these industries have been able to improve wage levels and enhance career opportunities for employees while keeping costs under control. For example, banks replace human tellers with automatic teller machines, which not only save labor costs but also offer 24-hour service year round. This kind of convenience provided to their customers can be considered a great customization.

ASSISTED LIVING INDUSTRY: NEW OPPORTUNITIES FOR HOSPITALITY

Assisted living represents a prime opportunity for hospitality companies willing to use the core competencies of hospitality to develop and operate communities for seniors. While most of the major hospitality entities have merged, consolidated or entered new market segments in last few years. only one hospitality company is currently a major player in the assisted living industry, Marriott International, which expanded into assisted living in 1989, now occupies the number two position on the chart for the top 25 U.S. Senior housing Owners and is ranked third in the top 25 U.S. Senior Housing Managers. In June of 1996, Marriott completed its merger with Forum Group, in the process acquiring an additional 42 assisted living facilities. As of October 1997, Marriott operated 82 assisted living communities, and the company plans to triple that number in the next five years.

Does Marriott's path in assisted living make sense for other hospitality companies? Clearly there are "cross-over" resources and skills between the hospitality and assisted living industries. Food and beverage and other processes in hospitality can be translated into assisted living operations. Indeed, hospitality companies with brands that represent service and quality have two of the most import ant ingredients when consumers make buying decisions in this industry. There are also challenges for a hospitality company expanding in this industry, however, given its mission of providing care services to the elderly. Nevertheless, the prospects may be attractive to hospitality companies with significant resources, given that assisted living is likely to be the fastest-growing segment in the long-term care industry.

Three primary demographic trends will shape growth of the assisted living industry in the next few decades. Advances in nutrition and medical science have resulted in an increased life expectancy, and consequently growing numbers of elderly people. Many seniors are living longer, more active lives.

Second, as an increasing number of women enter the workforce, their ability to serve as the primary caregiver to aging parents has been greatly reduced, thus changing the role of the family in providing elderly care. Third, a greater number of elderly are now living in isolation in many countries.

In the United States, for example, the average family moves once every five years. Many families are widely scattered, leaving elderly parents alone. Family structures have radically changed in recent decades. The end result is an elderly population that has been left without the traditional sources of assistance needed to perform their daily activities. Families must increasingly rely on alternative solutions to fulfill their previous roles as caregivers.

Proactive companies in the assisted living industry have stepped in to provide these services to a market that is forecast to grow at a record pace. The number of people aged 65 and over in the United States is currently 34 million, accounting for 13 percent of the total population. That number is projected to grow to 69 million, or 20 percent of the total population, by the year 2030.4 The number of elderly will only increase with the aging of the baby boom generation, those individuals born between 1946 and 1964. As this generation ages and retires, an increasing number of people over the age of 75 will require some level of care or assistance during the final years of their lives. The number of people aged 85 and over is currently 3.7 million and is projected to increase to 8.5 million by the year 2030. Demand will be driven by increases in how long people live. The average life expectancy for women aged 65 is projected to increase from 84.2 years in 1995 to 87.4 years in the year 2050.5

The demographic shift in the European Union (EU) may be even more extreme than in North America, where the demographic structure of society is more greatly influenced by immigration and slightly higher birth rates. The population aged 60 or over in the European Union had climbed by 50 percent in recent years, reaching 68.6 million by 1992. Estimates place the number of older people in the European Union at 80 to 100 million by the year 2020, of which 27 to 29 million are estimated to be over 80 years old. The average life expectancy in Europe is estimated at 78 years for men and 82.5 years for women. This is reported slightly lower in the United Kingdom at 77.6 years for men and 81.7 years for women.6

Also of urgent concern is the financial strength of the aging in the European Union, with poverty remaining a source of worry for many older people in EU countries. A 1993 Eurostate survey revealed that 48 percent of older people in the then 12 EU countries had financial difficulties.7 Health and social services or older people vary widely across Europe. Generally, however, the trend is toward de-emphasizing institutionalization and promoting private care or assistance. Although needs and resources vary greatly among the elderly in North America and Europe, assisted living will almost certainly sustain significant growth in the near future for a variety of reasons:

— Increased life expectancy of population as a whole, and of the assisted living target market;

— Decreased need for acute care by elderly;

— Increased relative wealth of elderly population;

— Decreased role of traditional substitutes to assisted living, particularly hospitals and nursing homes, as a result of cost pressures;

— Increased awareness and acceptance of assisted living services as an alternative to family care;

— Decreased lime available to traditional care providers, principally family members, creating the need for alternatives.

Inspired by the Dutch and Scandinavian systems, assisted living programs originally offered housing and sheltered services for the frail elderly. Today, the industry provides long-term care in a homelike environment at less expensive rates than nursing homes. Elderly residents gain an ability to live a more autonomous lifestyle, while enjoying the comfort and security of on-site services, including health programs and other types of support. As residents age, their level of need increases, and the community becomes responsible for providing more complex levels of care. This is commonly referred to as "aging in place." Residents are able to customize their level of care based upon their needs.

A Merrill Lynch industry report indicates that the average assisted living community comprises 58 separate private living units. A typical resident is a widowed or single female, 84 years of age, who needs assistance with three activities of daily living. Some 30 to 40 percent of residents suffer from Alzheimer's or some other form of dementia.

Due to the focus on lower acuity care, assisted living communities can offer the elderly the level of care that is individually required at prices that are typically two-thirds of what a nursing home would charge. Most assisted living communities in the United States offer a tiered pricing schedule in which residents pay a basic rate for room and board, and are then charged additional fees depending on the level of service they select.

This economic structure is beneficial for both the provider and the customer. The customer is able to obtain an individualized level of service at prices substantially less than at other higher acuity centers, like nursing homes. The provider is able to continuously serve customers as their needs change.

Assisted living companies in the United States are currently able to offer affordable services to their residents with monthly costs for assisted living (housing, meals and additional services) ranging from \$1,500 - \$3,000,9 with certain markets ranging as high as \$6,000 - \$7,000. Private payers represent 96 percent of the industry's total revenue. Costs to residents could increase substantially, however, depending on the extent of future regulation.

While U.S. nursing homes and other healthcare providers are heavily regulated on a federal level currently, the American assisted living industry is free of many of the costly compliance burdens of federal regulation. Regulation of the assisted living industry, however, looms on the horizon as the expansion of this industry has stimulated greater scrutiny of assisted living providers.

Opportunities for Hospitality

The assisted living industry is highly fragmented, with a growing trend toward consolidation. The supply of communities has been unable to keep pace with demand and consolidations have begun to accelerate. The top 50 operators in the industry housed an estimated 20 percent of the residents in 1996 until their needs required that they move to nursing homes or other higher acuity programs.10 Providers look to gain critical mass and strengthen their presence in particular geographic regions. This environment will create opportunities for strong operators and developers with loyal employees, an established marketing process, and access to capital.

The Competitive Landscape

Competition among companies in the assisted living industry exists on three levels - national, regional and local. To effectively compete on a national level, a company may need to have a strong brand name, access to sufficient capital and an ability to effectively execute appropriate development decisions. On a regional level, a company will need to take advantage of regional demographics, maximize efficient use of resources and establish brand equity. On a local level, competition varies widely. Factors influencing the local markets include geographic location, knowledge of the elderly population trends currently and going forward, and regulatory issues. Also critical are supply-and-demand forces shaping the local market in its current phase and what is expected for the future.

Marketeting to Customers

To effectively position companies within key markets, it is essential to understand the distinction between the prospective resident of the assisted living community and the customer who may be an adult child caring for an aging parent. In the assisted living industry, there are unique challenges to target and market to the consumer (the potential resident of the assisted living facility). The customer, however, may be the adult child who is the primary caregiver. Most residents - or their family caregivers - choose an assisted living community within a certain radius of their family. This highlights the importance of careful target marketing to identify not only the demographics of the resident, but also of the family.

Access to Capital

As competition continues to increase, access to capital will be a major factor in success. Currently, the ability to obtain capital in the public and private markets in the United States is at an unprecedented level as investors recognize the opportunities and returns of the assisting living market. Within The last 24 months, there have been 16 public equity offerings, six convertible offerings and multiple REIT financings by assisted living companies in the United States. In a capital-constrained environment, those companies with access to capital through relationships with strategic partners will have a competitive advantage. Again, strong hospitality entities would be able to supplement local assisted living operators.

Competitive and Market Conclusions

The fundamentals driving the assisted living industry - including the aging of populations in advanced economies and the drive to better manage health care costs - will continue to provide exceptional demand for assisted living services. Given the industry's fundamentals, a company with access to capital, strategic focus and commitment to operational excellence should be well positioned to be a leader in the market. As competition in this evolving market increases, consolidation will provide companies with an opportunity to expand both within their own niche of service and into other levels of the care continuum.

Although hospitality companies may have the brand equity and the operational expertise of running a housing community, it is essential for them to provide the other health - and support - related services to elderly residents. Residents of assisted living communities require more services than a hotel guest. That is the core difference between hospitality and assisted living. Competitors for elderly residents offer communities and services at all points of the senior care continuum, from skilled nursing communities and acute care hospitals, to companies providing home-based health care. Hospitality companies considering the assisted living market may want to consider partnerships with current operators. The hospitality companies can offer critical mass, brand reputation and general operational expertise, while the care-giving expertise would be provided by the assisted living company.

The prospects for providers of assisted living housing look extremely promising. The number of potential customers is rapidly rising, and they can be expected to have lengthy stays at assisted living communities. At the same time, there is currently a limited supply of assisted living communities. This all translates into opportunities for proactive companies. The hospitality industry may be one of the beneficiaries.

Bibliography

Cohen, E., "Toward a Sociology of International Tourism," *Social Research*, 39:164-182, 1972.

Airey, D, and Nightingale, M., "Tourism occupations, career profile and knowledge", *Annals of Tourism Research*, 8(1), 1981.

_____________ and Tribe, J., "Hospitality education", in C. Lashley and A. Morrison (eds.) *In Search of Hospitality: Theoretical Perspectives and Debates*, Oxford, Butterworth Heinemann, 2000

Baum, T., and Nickson, D., "Teaching human resource management in hospitality and tourism: a critique", *International Journal of Contemporary Hospitality Management*, 10: 75-79, 1998.

Doxey, G., "When Enough's Enough: The Natives are Restless in Old Niagara," *Heritage Canada*, 2(2):26-27, 1976.

Dwyer, L., P. Forsyth, J. Madden, and R. Spurr, *Economic Impacts of Inbound Tourism under Different Assumptions, Regarding the Macroeconomy, Current Issues in Tourism*, 3: 325-363, 2000.

Fletcher, J.E., "Input-Output Analysis and Tourism Impact Studies", *Annals of Tourism Research 16*: 514-529, 1989.

Gartner, William C., "Environmental Impacts of Recreational Home Developments", *Annals of Tourism Research 14*: 38-57, 1987.

______________ and David W. Lime, *Trends in Outdoor Recreation, Leisure and Tourism,* Wallingford:CABI Publishing (on reserve in Tourism Center), 2000.

Gartner, W. C., *Tourism Development: Principles, Processes, Policies*. New York: Van Nostrand Reinhold, 1996.

Hardin, G., "The Tragedy of the Commons," *Science,* 162:1243-1248, 1968.

Irwin, P., W. Gartner, and C. Phelps, "Mexican-American/ Anglo Cultural Differences as Recreation Style Determinants," *Leisure Studies*, 12:335-348, 1990.

Jafari, J., "Retrospective and Prospective Views on Tourism as Field of Study", *Paper presented at the 1988 Meeting of the Academy of Leisure Sciences*, Indianapolis, Indiana, 1988.

McIntosh, R,. C. Goeldner and B. Ritchie, *"Tourism: Principles, Practices, Philosophies*, 7 th ed. New York: John Wiley and Sons, Inc., 1994.

Murphy, P., *"Tourism: A Community Approach*. New York: Metheun, 1985.

Shanklin, Carol W., "Ecology Age: Implications for the Hospitality and Tourism Industry", *Hospitality Research Journal: The Professional Journal of the Council on Hotel, Restaurant, and Institutional Education, 17* (1), 219-229.

Index